A Year of Walks in SUSSEX

Roy Woodcock

Published by Sigma Leisure – an imprint of
Sigma Press, 1 South Oak Lane, Wilmslow, Cheshire SK9 6AR, England.

British Library Cataloguing in Publication Data
A CIP record for this book is available from the British Library.

ISBN: 1-85058-609-8

Typesetting and Design by: Sigma Press, Wilmslow, Cheshire.

Cover photographs, clockwise, from top left: near Stoughton; Bosham; Southease church; Clayton windmills

Maps: based on original artwork supplied by the author
Drawings: Wendy Galassini
Photographs: the author

Printed by: MFP Design and Print

Disclaimer: the information in this book is given in good faith and is believed to be correct at the time of publication. No responsibility is accepted by either the author or publisher for errors or omissions, or for any loss or injury howsoever caused. Only you can judge your own fitness, competence and experience.

Preface

This collection of circular walks visits 12 outstanding locations in Sussex and crosses delightful countryside in all of them. The walks are not rugged or arduous, but more for walkers seeking fresh air and exercise whilst seeing the county in all its moods throughout the year. The choice of walks is inevitably personal, but these are certainly interesting locations, including seven in the Downs. Most parts of the county are scenically attractive and there are two Areas of Outstanding Natural Beauty, the South Downs and the High Weald. The walks are from 6 to 16 miles long and can be taken as a full day out, but each of them has a short cut alternative of between 5 and 9 miles. This enables walkers to choose a shorter or more leisurely outing, which may suit families with small children. There are always features of interest on the walks, whether it is a nature reserve with flowers or birds, an old church, the local geology, local history or links with famous writers.

It is hoped that references to the weather, the landscape and the features of natural history which might be seen or experienced in each month will add to the pleasure, interest and enjoyment of each walk. The features of natural history mentioned are generally those which are likely to be seen during the walk, not the rare or shy for which a lengthy wait may be required. It is hoped that the walks will enable you to discover features of the landscape which perhaps had not been noticed before, and to appreciate the countryside as it changes through the year. Each month has its own particular attractions, but although the walks specifically refer to a particular month, they can all be enjoyed at any time of the year.

Roy Woodcock

Acknowledgements

My major thanks are to Margaret for accompanying me on all the walks, and then spending many hours checking the text for accuracy. Many thanks to Wendy Galassini for her delightful drawings of buildings and natural history subjects, which portray some of the features to be seen on the walks, as well as brightening up the text. I am grateful for responses to letters of enquiry sent to the National Trust Regional Office at Slindon and the Sussex Downs Conservation Board in Storrington, as well as answers to my questions at many of the Tourist Information Centres in the county.

Contents

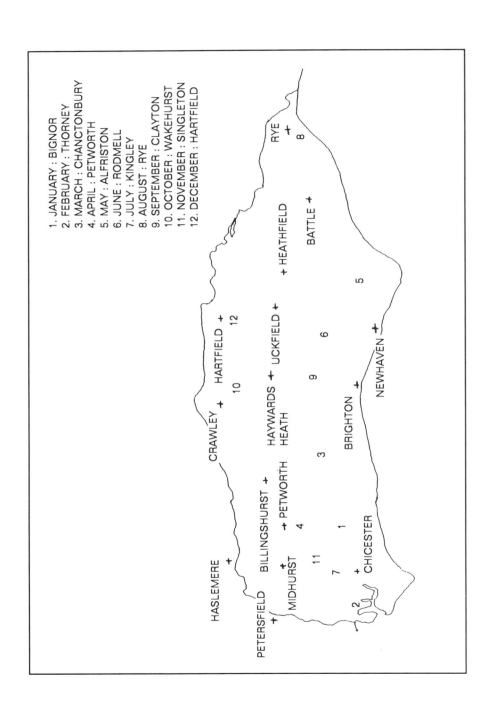

1. JANUARY : BIGNOR
2. FEBRUARY : THORNEY
3. MARCH : CHANCTONBURY
4. APRIL : PETWORTH
5. MAY : ALFRISTON
6. JUNE : RODMELL
7. JULY : KINGLEY
8. AUGUST : RYE
9. SEPTEMBER : CLAYTON
10. OCTOBER : WAKEHURST
11. NOVEMBER : SINGLETON
12. DECEMBER : HARTFIELD

Introduction

The County of Sussex consists of two administrative areas, East Sussex with its county town at Lewes, and West Sussex with its county town in Chichester. East Sussex has an area of 179 530 hectares and West Sussex is slightly larger, covering an area of 198 935 hectares. Each of these two regions has a population of just over 700 000.

The landscape

The two administrative areas together have a long west-east extent, and both contain a coastline along the English Channel. This coastline is lined with beaches and holiday resorts, some of which are also retirement towns. Inland are the chalk hills of the South Downs, running roughly parallel to the coast but ending at Beachy Head near Eastbourne. North of the chalk hills are clay lowlands, and further north still are sandstone ridges which extend from near Black Down Hills in the west, just south of Haslemere, to the Ashdown Forest and the Harrison Rocks or High Rocks close to Tunbridge Wells.

These different rocks were originally nearly horizontal, as they accumulated on the bed of the sea more than 100 million years ago, in the Cretaceous period. Earth movements which formed the Alps crumpled these sediments into a huge ridge, which was highest in the middle of the Weald and sloped down gradually to the English Channel and the Thames valley. Rivers began to flow from this ridge, both to north and to the south, carving valleys and contributing to the general erosion of the ridge to its present form.

Because of this geological history, the oldest rocks are the sandstones in the middle of the Weald, and moving north or south will give a similar sequence of rocks, mostly clays or sandstones. The most northerly rock of the Weald is the chalk of the North Downs, and the most southerly rock of the Weald is the chalk of the South Downs. These areas of chalk are very similar because they were originally both part of the same layer (stratum) of chalk which was the top of the ridge. All the chalk which formerly covered the entire Weald has been eroded during the last 50 million years.

It is only the South Downs which are in Sussex, and they have been crossed by four rivers: the Cuckmere, Ouse, Adur and Arun, which rise in the middle of the Weald and flow southwards to the sea, cutting gaps through the chalk on their way. The South Downs have been designated an Area of Outstanding Natural Beauty (see the June walk).

The clay areas, which are generally the lowest and contain the heaviest soils, have been used for farming, whereas much of the sandstone, where the soils are acid and poorer in nutrient, has remained as forest or heathland. Parts of the chalk hills are still covered by grassland, though most has been used for arable crops in recent decades. There is now a slight reversal of this trend because of overproduction of food in Europe and increasing attempts to attract wild life to the Downs and restore more of the original grassland.

The chalk forms a very distinctive landscape, with a north-facing escarpment and a more gentle, south-facing dip slope. This shape, known as a cuesta, is the result of the geological evolution of the area, and subsequent erosion. The chalk forms many impressive cliffs along the coast, notably at Beachy Head and the Seven Sisters between Birling and the Cuckmere.

On the dip slope are many dry valleys with ridges between them, and these produce a wave-like landscape. Richard Jefferies, writing about the Downs in the 1880s, said that 'all the ridges and slopes seem alike, and there is no end to them'.

The valleys were cut by rivers sometime in the past, probably when the land was frozen solid during the Ice Age, and formed a landscape similar to the Tundra of northern Canada or northern Sweden today. At that time the permafrost, or permanently frozen ground, prevented water from percolating downwards, and consequently it flowed on the surface as rivers during the summer, when temperatures were above freezing point. As the climate warmed up and the ground thawed out, the water was able to sink underground into the porous chalk and so the valleys became dry. Water will only appear on the surface in these valleys when the ground is saturated and the water table is very high.

Another landscape feature dating from colder climatic conditions is to be seen on the escarpment, where many steep-sided hollows can be seen (see the May walk). These are vaguely similar to giant arm chairs and are called coombes, or if they are covered with trees may be called hangers. They were formed by freezing and thawing of the ground in colder climatic times, when the top soil and loose rocks were eroded and gradually slithered downhill, to accumulate at the foot of the slope. The hollows created by this activity are carved or scalloped into the scarp. Their shape is quite similar to that of corries, though these were formed by glaciers and ice action, not by freezing and thawing.

Farming and settlements

The Downs were originally forested when Man first moved into the area, and it was probably the Neolithic farmers who began to clear the forest. They would have found the chalk uplands safer from attack than the neighbouring lowlands, and would also have found the forest easier to clear than the denser forest down on the clay soils. The light, chalky soils were easier to work with primitive tools and so provided a preferable area for settlement.

Settlement probably began before 3000BC, and by 1000BC cereals were being grown in many places. Simple ox-drawn ploughs were used, and continued turning of the soil would allow soil to slip downhill, thereby creating the low banks or lynchets round the fields. Arable farming was particularly important in Roman times, but farming declined in subsequent centuries and by the Middle Ages sheep farming was the main activity. This remained the most important type of farming from the 14th century until the First World War, when more ploughing began to take place, as had happened on a small scale in Napoleonic times. The amount of ploughland increased dramatically in the Second World War, and reversal of this process has been seen only in the last decade.

All parts of Sussex are influenced by London and are crossed by many roads and railways linking London with the coast and many residential towns and villages in Sussex. In spite of this, there are numerous areas of countryside and an abundance of public footpaths, and it is always possible to get away from the built-up areas and roads.

Weather

The weather in the county is as varied as in all parts of England, but has a few of its own local characteristics. Many of the sandy and slightly higher areas of the north are covered by trees, which provide shelter in winter, and shade in summer. The higher hills are the South Downs and these are often covered by grassland or plough and these are very exposed to winds, and can be bitterly cold in winter. These low hills create a barrier between the coastal areas and the inland, and the weather on the coast can be quite different from that north of the Downs. The Downs themselves experience more frost, snow and cloud than the land to the north or south.

Average weather conditions are shown by the way in which the flowers grow in spring, trees become green and then shed their leaves in autumn, and crops grow successfully through the summer months. All this is in spite of the weekly and daily variations for which the British climate is noted.

The mean average temperature in south-eastern England is about 10°C. January is the coldest month, except on the coast where February may have a lower mean temperature. Average minimum temperatures on the coast are about 2°C as compared with 0.5°C inland. Frost is rare on the coast, and whereas Eastbourne has six air frosts and 12 ground frosts in an average January, Gatwick further inland has figures of 13 and 17. Sunshine totals are amongst the highest in Britain, with an average annual total of about 1800 hours near the coast, and 1600 inland. The annual average for Eastbourne is 1827 hours.

Rainfall totals range from 700 to 1000mm per annum, with Littlehampton on the coast receiving 730mm and Plumpton at the foot of the Downs averaging 1016mm. Snowfall tends to be slight in Sussex, and there are an average of 10 days with snow or sleet falling on the coast and about 20 on the higher ground inland. Snow lying amounts to about six days near the coast and 15 inland, where an increase of about 100 metres in height causes an increase of about five days of snow.

The Walks

Each walk is accompanied by a map, and together with the detailed description of the walk this should enable anyone to find and follow the route. However, it will be useful to have the 1:25 000 Ordnance Survey Explorer or 1:50 000 OS Landranger maps in case of problems with the route. 'Explorer' maps are gradually replacing the older Pathfinder maps (both are at the same scale) and all Pathfinders will be repaced by Explorers by the year 2003. OS maps also provide information and detail about the surrounding area. It is always advisable to carry a compass, which can be especially useful in woodlands or in fog, when sense of direction may be lost.

Month	Short Cut (miles)	Full Walk (miles)	OS Landranger (1:50 000) map(s)	OS Pathfinder (1:25 000) map(s)	OS Explorer (1:25 000) map(s)
January	6	8	197	1286/1287	121
February	8	16	197	1304	120
March	5	12	198	1287/1306	121
April	7	8	197	1266/1286	133/121
May	9	14.5	198/199	1308	123
June	9	13	198	1307/1308	122
July	7.5	8.5	197	1286/1305	120
August	8	10.5	189	1271/1291	125
September	7	9	198	1288	122
October	6	9	187	1247	135
November	5	6	197	1286	120
December	7	9.5	188	1248	135

Many places will be muddy, especially in winter, and some sections of the walks are steep or stony, therefore, boots are advisable. It is also advisable, or even essential, to carry windproof and waterproof clothing, as well as a warm drink and some food if going out all day, even though there are locations for refreshment on most of the walks described. Any steep climbs are referred to in the description, as are any locations which might be available for refreshment.

Binoculars are very handy, especially if you are at all interested in bird life, and they sometimes help to pinpoint the location of stiles at the opposite side of a field. Cameras, too, are useful, as all the walks contain many photogenic locations.

All details were correct at the time of walking. All the walks follow public rights of way, and were free from obstructions at the time of last walking the routes described.

January: Bignor

This walk is through woods and farmland, and up and then down the north-facing escarpment, at the foot of which will be seen a spring. Evidence of the Roman invasion of Britain is encountered in Bignor and on Bignor Hill.

Distance: 8 miles, with a short cut route of 6 miles.

Time: 4 hours (3 hours)

Terrain: Gently undulating except for the steep slope of the South Downs escarpment

Maps: Explorer 121 or Landranger 197.

Starting Point: The large car park at Whiteways roundabout, where the A29 is met by the B2139 coming from Storrington and the A284 from

Snowdrops

Arundel. GR 002119. The picnic site has toilets and a small snack bar.

Access: A bus service links Arundel with nearby towns along the A27, and Arundel has a railway station.

Refreshments: Only at the start.

Nearest Town: Arundel, which also has a Tourist Information Centre (tel. 01903 882268).

Weather

'As the days lengthen, so the cold strengthens.' Sadly this is often true, as the worst of the winter is not yet over. The official three months of winter are December, January and February, so spring is still far off, in spite of the good cheer of the gradually lengthening hours of daylight. Another old country saying about January has the same message – the worst weather is yet to come, which is often, though not invariably, true.

January is the coldest month of the year, except for some coastal areas where February is slightly colder. Even so there can be mild days if Atlantic weather is dominant, and this will generally last for a week or more. Spells of colder weather can be varied in harshness, but if the air is from Europe or Siberia it will feel bitterly cold, and can be especially unpleasant in Kent and Sussex. Average temperatures in January are about 7°C in Cornwall, but about 4°C in Sussex. Snow is not recorded in Sussex every year, but there can be exceptional conditions. January 1997 was the driest since 1779 and was colder than average. It began with a very cold spell of easterly weather and there were a few days when the maximum temperature did not rise above minus 2°C. The year began with a snow cover, which persisted for the first ten days, and up to 12.5cms (5ins) of snow had fallen in places. Compare this with 1947 when drifts in south-eastern England reached up to 8 metres, and did not really thaw until mid-March.

The Countryside

The advantages of walking in January are the more distant views and the ease with which it is possible to see birds. There are no flies or brambles or nettles, but there is likely to be mud or frost, and most serious of all is the shortage of daylight. In the chalky areas of the South Downs, perhaps rather surprisingly on a porous rock, the mud is very slippery and is very clingy, making boots heavier and heavier.

The walk to Bignor encounters several typical features of the chalkland landscape, with the steep north-facing scarp, and the more gentle dip slope where the walk begins and finishes. The steep scarp overlooking Bignor is scalloped by the eroded hollows called coombes, and much of the steep slope is covered with woodlands.

These wooded slopes are often referred to as hangers here in the South Downs, and also in the Chilterns and near Selborne, the home of the famous 18th-century naturalist Gilbert White.

In these and other woodlands, this is a month when foresters are working in the woods, cutting down and thinning, and in several places you may see the neatly stacked piles of trunks and logs awaiting collection. Wholesale clearance does not normally take place as most British woodlands are managed in a sustainable way, to bring in some regular income each year, and also maintain the woodland as an amenity.

Outside the woods, the grassy fields are dull and only contain very short grass, not able to provide much grazing. Most of the cattle are indoors at this time of year. The arable fields are still bare or have been recently ploughed, except for a few sown in autumn with cereal crops or winter vegetables and now showing a few centimetres of young, green growth. Very few fields of stubble remain over the winter nowadays, a sad loss to the finches, skylarks and partridges, which used to find precious items of food in the remnants of last year's crops.

Winter walking may have to contend with snow and ice, or wet and windy weather, which seem to be the only alternatives at this time of year. The snow and ice, in association with the bright sunshine can give exhilarating walks and magnificent views and the best of wintry conditions. The wet and windy has less to recommend it except for milder temperatures, which on occasions can reach 15C, similar to the coolest days experienced in July. However, choice of day is important for any winter walk, and the route followed for this January walk involves one or two exposed places. Be prepared, with good clothing and a piping hot flask of tea or coffee in the rucksack.

South Downs Way

This is the only long-distance path which is open to horse riders and cyclists. Designated in 1972, it extended from Beachy Head near Eastbourne to the Queen Elizabeth Country Park and Butser Hill alongside the A3 south of Petersfield, but there is now an extension to Winchester. The total length is 106 miles, and it is walked by the very energetic in five or six days. It is possible to take a train for the return journey.

The South Downs Way on Bignor Hill

Bignor Roman Villa

Generally open from March till October, the villa was rediscovered in 1811 when George Tupper, the local farmer, moved a stone whilst ploughing, and exposed part of the remarkable mosaic floors. The long mosaic in the north corridor is 24 metres (80ft), the longest on display anywhere in the country, and includes the noted Venus and Gladiator mosaic. The villa was probably occupied from the 1st to the 4th centuries. Excavations near the villa have shown that the thin, chalky soils in this area have been cultivated for thousands of years. Excavation work still continues.

Bignor Hill

Bignor Hill is part of the 1400-hectare (3500 acres) Slindon Estate, a gift to the National Trust from Mr J.F. Wooton Isaacson in 1950. The estate contains several archaeological sites, including the Neolithic causeway camp at Barkhale, just to the south.

Stane Street

This Roman road was metalled and cambered, and generally 7.6 me-

tres (25ft) wide. It was built of flint layers in gravel and chalk, with a
ditch and bank alongside. Traces of the drainage ditches can still be
seen in places. The raised metalled bed, the Agger, was between 6
and 15 metres (20 to 50ft) in width. The road is very straight from
Chichester to Pulborough, but a branch road went down the scarp
here to the important villa at Bignor. The National Trust owns 3¾
miles of Stane Street. Most of the Roman route from London to
Chichester has disappeared, and some of it is followed by the A285
from Chichester and the A29 from Pulborough to Billingshurst. Noviomagus Regnensium was the Roman name for Chichester, and the
important port of Fishbourne was linked to London via Stane Street.
Imagine the Roman soldiers marching along here in January – quite
a contrast with weather conditions back home in Rome.

Bignor church

The Walk

Walk northwards out of the car park (1), with the A29 on your right, to follow the left-hand side of the field for three-quarters of a mile. There may be gulls and rooks in evidence, especially if there has been recent ploughing in the field to the right. This is a hard time of the year for the birds, and they need to be alert to any opportunity for finding food. As the path descends slightly, views open up left, over Houghton Forest, which extends over 254 hectares, and is looked after by the Forestry Commission.

At a major cross-paths, pick up the well-worn track of the South Downs Way, along which you turn westwards through large, open fields, which can become very windswept. Small patches of soil and green shoots of the summer cereal crop protrude between the thousands of stones littering the fields. It is amazing that this thin and stony soil can produce the golden fields of cereals to be seen in this area in the summer. Changing patterns of farming in recent years have seen more fields of grass and set-aside land, as the number of cereal fields has declined. A century ago, the whole of this landscape was covered by grass, but it was increasingly ploughed up for cereals from the time of the First World War. The recent surpluses of food in Europe have seen a return to less intensive arable farming, and a greater variety in the farming, including some sheep farming, though not on the scale of former times.

A mile of open fields ends with the slow descent into a dry valley running along the left side of the path. The large barns alongside the path will provide welcome shelter for a picnic lunch if the time is right and the weather is harsh. There are pheasants around this area and you are likely to see a winter flock of skylarks flitting around in the bare fields. Skylarks are one of several varieties of bird which gang together in flocks during the winter.

Short Cut

Five paths meet here (2) and the main route goes straight ahead, following the signpost to the Roman Villa. For the short cut walk, take the path just to the left of straight ahead. This is the South Downs Way, and from the three barns it goes left for about 10 metres. and then right along a broad and well-worn track running parallel with the straight ahead route. After 30 metres the track bends left and be-

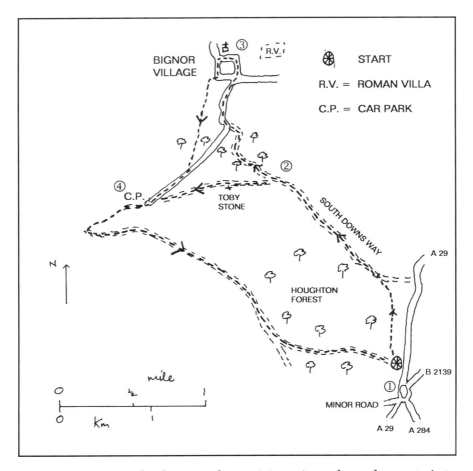

gins a fairly steep climb. It reaches a T-junction where the route is to the right, following the blue arrow, and continues to climb, with good views opening up to the north (right) including an almost aerial view looking down on the Roman villa. The Toby Stone is a memorial located at the National Trust sign for the beginning of the Bignor Hill property.

Toby was James Wentworth Fitzwilliam (1888-1955), Secretary Cowdray Hounds 1922-1930, British Fields Sports Society1930-1953, Master of Fox Hounds Association 1945-1955. The inscription is 'Here he lies where he longed to be'.

Beyond the Toby Stone, the top of the climb is soon reached, the highest point of Bignor Hill (738ft) being just to the right of the path, and then a steady descent leads to the small car parking area, where the main route is rejoined (4).

Longer Route

From the junction of five paths (2), we go straight ahead in a north-westerly direction, up into the woods, following the signpost to the Roman Villa. The trees are mainly deciduous with a few yew and laurel.

The winding track leads down through the trees clothing the steep scarp slopes (a hanger), and we turn right on the narrow road linking the village with the National Trust car park up on the hill. The scarp is 525ft (160 metres) high, but at the foot are green fields on the clay, with the delightful view of Bignor village as we emerge from the trees. The large barns of a farm in the village, a few thatched houses, the tiny church and the Roman villa can all be seen.

The road into the village is joined by a small stream rising from a spring beneath the chalk. At the T-junction turn right and then immediately left (following the signpost to Sutton and Duncton). Walk round the village along a rectangular route, but you may wish to detour on the 'No Through Road' to the right as this leads to the Roman villa.

Retrace your steps to the road and continue the circuit of the village, passing the stone buildings of Manor Farm, the headquarters for the Vacances en Campagne and Vacanze in Italia holiday company, the Individual Travellers' Company.

A little further along the road is the small church of Holy Cross (3) which had Norman ancestry and was mentioned in the Domesday Book. It was mostly rebuilt in the 13th century though the Norman chancel arch remains, and further restoration took place in 1876-78. A traditional yew tree stands in the churchyard. Leave the church beneath the lych-gate and take the road opposite, going slightly downhill to walk along another part of the village. A small terrace of stone cottages sits simply behind a flint wall. Across the road from these are snowdrops growing on the bank. Turn right over a ford and then left to follow the small stream. Go over stiles and alongside the left side of the fields as the path follows the small stream past a pond with moorhens to the spring, where the cold, clear water emerges from beneath the chalk. The final field up to the wooded scarp may still contain jumps and obstacles for showjumping training and practice.

Enter the woods, cross over the track and follow a path diagonally up through the wood. Many fallen trees are reminders of massive devastation by the gales of recent years, but nature has amazing ability to recover and much new growth will soon replace the dead trees. Some signs of old coppicing can be seen, but many of the hazels are growing catkins to give an early hint of spring. Beech leaves and mast line many sections of the path, and in places dog's mercury is appearing through the debris on the ground. This is a lovely walk up through the woods. There are views out across the fields and on to the next hill with its radio masts which would not be visible in the summer months.

At the narrow road turn right and continue up to Bignor Hill and the National Trust car park (4) and picnic spot, a delightful location for a summer picnic, but not a place for sitting around in January. The signpost indicates Noviomagus is to the south-west, Bignor and Londinium to the east.

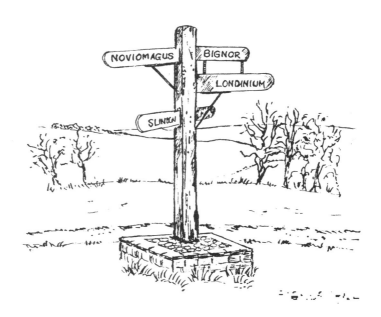

Several paths meet at the signpost, including the short cut route, and we take the track leading westwards towards the radio masts. After about 150 metres, we reach a National Trust information board, which tells us that this is Stane Street, a Roman road constructed about AD70 to connect Fishbourne Harbour, near Chichester, with London.

Turn left along Stane Street, following in the footsteps of the Romans for about 200 metres, to where the South Downs Way track bends to the right. Stay on Stane Street as it begins to descend and notice the good views right, across the South Downs Way and up to the masts. Just before reaching the stile, turn left and follow the bridleway going into a small wood. Once through the wood we reach a track, with Blackjack down to the right, but we go straight ahead on a broad track with trees to the left and an open field to the right. The very flinty field on the right slopes down gently. A seat on the left is a good place for the views out towards the coast near Bognor, and the small wood on the left provides shelter from north winds. Keep straight on, passing a cross-tracks and another seat before arriving at a major cross-tracks, where the car park on Bignor Hill is up to the left. Go straight ahead here, with a wood on the right and a field on the left which is the site of the Barkhale Neolithic camp. Molehills abound here, as elsewhere on the Downs. They may be developing flattened noses as a result of pushing up new molehills littered with numerous stones, which must create difficulties for them when digging new tunnels.

Beyond the open field there are woods on both sides of the path, and we walk south-eastwards into Houghton Forest. A well-marked track leads south-east for a mile and then bends in an easterly direction back to the car park. The woods contain many patches where widespread devastation can be seen, resulting from the gales of 1987 and 1990. Much clearance work has been completed and replanting too, but recovery will be slow and spread over decades rather than years. There are areas of commercial clearing too. Many of the surviving trees are beech, and some blocks of coniferous, but not large spreads of dark evergreens.

Open patches, which may contain gorse in flower even at this time of year, together with the mixture of deciduous and evergreens, contributes to a rich bird life in this area. Goldcrests can be seen and heard, thrushes and blackbirds, many finches and blue, great, long-tailed and willow or marsh tits. (I can never distinguish the last two from each other, without watching for a long time waiting for call notes to be uttered.) Wrens are scuttling around in the undergrowth, and occasionally making a loud noise, shouting at other wrens nearby. Treecreepers will be working their way up one tree trunk, like little mice, before flying down to a neighbouring tree to continue the never-ending search for insects.

The shelter of the woods may provide a welcome relief after the exposed sections of the walk earlier, but soon the noise of traffic along the main road will be heard, and a return to the noisy and crowded world will be inevitable as we approach the car park to complete the walk.

February: Chichester Harbour

The walk stays close to the shore of Chichester Harbour, a shallow inlet of the sea, with low islands and peninsulas protruding into the water. At high tide the harbour is all water, often crowded with small boats, but at low tide the vast expanses of mud are used by thousands of birds as feeding grounds.

Brent Geese

Distance: 16 miles, with a short cut of 8 miles.

Time: About 7 hours (or 3 to 4 hours for the shorter walk).

Terrain: Flat, but can become very muddy. There are occasional stiles on the Thorney stretch of the walk.

Map: Explorer 120 or Landranger 197.

Starting Point: Emsworth (GR 749046), which can be reached along the A259, off the A27 between Portsmouth and Chichester.

Access: Bus services and trains run to Emsworth from Chichester and Havant.

Refreshments: Available in Emsworth and there is a pub in Chidham.

Nearest Town: Emsworth

Nearest Tourist Information Centre: Chichester (tel. 01243 775888)

Weather

Although February weather can be very variable, there is normally at least one mild spell and also one cold spell. One of the earliest writers to mention spells of weather was Alexander Buchan, a member of the Scottish Meteorological Society, who recorded a regular cold spell between 7th and 14th of February. His analysis was based only on ten years' records in Scotland, and although the idea is correct, the actual timing will vary from year to year. A harsh spell of weather must be expected, especially on a low, exposed coastline such as in Chichester Harbour. The sea is still very cool, and contributes to making this the coldest month in coastal areas.

The old rhyme about Candlemas Day (2nd February) is:

> *'If Candlemas Day be fair and bright,*
> *Winter will have another flight.*
> *If Candlemas Day be cloud and rain,*
> *Then winter will not come again.'*

Anyone forecasting the entire month as early as the second day is likely to be incorrect, with the changeable nature of British weather. There is always the likelihood of a mild spell, when westerly weather brings wind and rain, and this will encourage the early growth of spring flowers.

Many of the old Saints' days have weather sayings associated with them, but they tend to be very gloomy and just mention the worst of the weather possibilities. For example, St Dorothy (February 6th) is said to bring the snow – which it might do in an occasional year, but it will not be a reliable forecast.

The Countryside

Chichester Harbour is low and flat, and exposed to the wind. The only shelter is from the Downs to the north or from occasional clumps of low trees. Easterly winds are likely to be the most bitter, westerlies may be stronger but milder, though they can be raw. Impressive and dramatic skies can be seen, which are very popular with artists and photographers, with a large number of boats adding to the general appearance of the scene. A good anorak is vital for this walk, especially as the wealth of bird life will encourage frequent stops, to stand and look. This is a real bird watcher's walk, so do not forget your binoculars.

Bleak it may be, but the birds love it, and many plants will be growing in the mud on the shore margins as well as in the marshy areas of the land. Reed-beds are common, and on the grasslands many wildflowers, including some orchids, grow in the spring and summer. Water is an important part of the landscape, even on land, as it is never far below the surface. Crops grow well in summer, but the water table is generally too high for anything other than water-loving plants to be seen in February.

Birds include true land birds, notably the rare short-eared owl, which hunts in daytime and can often be seen here, as well as brent-geese which graze in grassy areas, and also kingfishers and herons. But the real wealth is on the mud – a rich source of food, exposed twice every 24 hours, with its supplies renewed. Ducks (mallard, teal, sheld) and waders (redshank, oyster catcher, dunlin) are numerous.

Any mild days will be accompanied by an ever-growing amount of birdsong, and bees will start to move if the temperatures go above

Bosham

10C. A few trees may also show signs of life, notably the sallow, which bursts forth with small furry catkins, and the lambs' tails on the hazel will brighten up from their dull, winter colouring.

Chichester Harbour

The inlets of the harbour are expanses of mud at low tide, and very popular for wading birds, ducks and geese. The shores have a unique assortment of plants, which find their own perfect locations dependent on their ability to grow in different habitats. Wind, birds and sails are constant companions whilst walking round the flat, exposed landscape of the harbour. Beware of high spring tides. These come up on to the path in a couple of locations, and may delay your walk for an hour or so. (Telephone the Harbour Master on 01243 512301 for details.)

Thorney Island

Thorney Island was joined to the mainland in 1870, when 72 hectares (178 acres) of land were reclaimed. The channel called Great Deep is where the island used to begin.

Pilsey Island

If you can time your arrival here to coincide with high tide (information on tides available from the Chichester Harbour Master) in any of the winter months, there will be a real wealth of bird life to look at. When the sea covers their feeding grounds, thousands of birds come to Pilsey Island to rest, until they can resume their never-ending search for food when the tide goes out and exposes the mud again. Geese, curlews, dunlin, godwits, grey plover, sheld duck, oyster catchers and others can be seen.

Nutbourne Marshes

Nutbourne Marshes Nature Reserve occupies 365 hectares (900 acres) of intertidal mud between Chidham and Thorney. The two small islands of North and South Stakes are remnants of attempts in the 1870s to reclaim an area of marsh. These two small, low islands provide a home for nesting terns and several varieties of wading birds. Marsh plants such as sea purslane, sea thrift and sea lavender grow well in summer, but many plants will be evident even in February.

The Walk

Start from the car park in the centre of Emsworth (1). To the right along South Street is the sea and an old tidal mill now used by the local sailing club, but for our walk we turn left along South Street and into The Square, where there is a useful information board and map. Turn right along High Street for a few metres, and then left along Queen Street to pass the old flour mill on the left, and Dolphin Quay on the right. Just past the Lord Raglan, turn right through a small, new development on to a footpath which is alongside the Slipper Mill Pool. Here there are likely to be gulls, most of which will be black-headed gulls, though in winter plumage they will be showing only two black spots rather than a complete dark brown head. There are sometimes coots and possibly dabchicks and red-breasted merganser on this pool.

Turn left at the end of the pool, and then right alongside the Slipper Mill (2), to walk straight ahead and through the marina, following the footpath sign. Pass between boats, many of which will be having winter maintenance work done on them in preparation for the spring and summer sailing. At the end of the harbour area, turn right to walk along the driveway between more boats, and reach the sea wall, with views to Hayling Island. Turn left to walk southwards, passing the chalets on stilts on the left, and listen to the bird noises on the right. Perhaps there will be the continuous grunting and gurgling of the geese, or piping of the oyster catchers or the distinctive call of the curlew – there will also be the noise of the wind.

Just beyond the last of these chalets is a Countryside Commission Information Board about Chichester Harbour and Thorney Island, with several drawings of plants and birds which might be seen. The terns are mentioned, though they are here only in the summer, and also the red-breasted merganser, brent-geese, and many waders. A brief history of Thorney and the two inlets, Great Deep and Little Deep, is given, as well as an explanation of how to gain access to the coastal path further south along Thorney coast. Of the plants which may be seen, glasswort grows nearest to the seawater, and then on slightly higher ground are sea purslane and sea lavender. The cord grass (spartina) which grows on the mud flats has decreased in recent years.

Go on beyond the chalets on stilts and keep going southwards

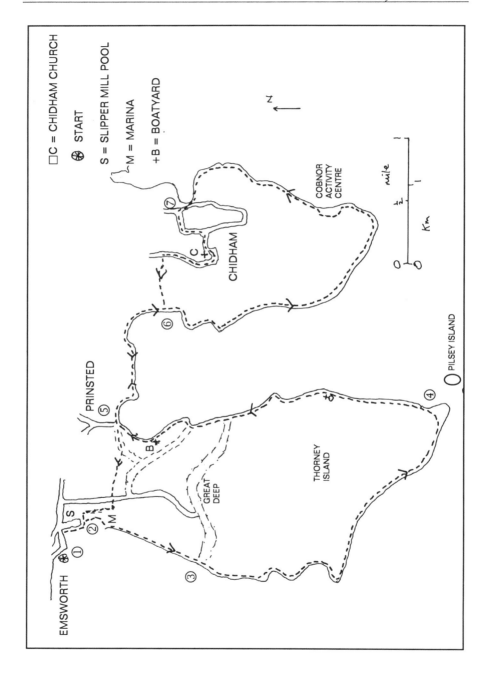

along the sea wall. To the left is a channel, and beyond this is the reed and
marsh area of the Little Deep. This reed
and pond environment on the left is rich
in bird life in the summer, and the mud
or sea to the right is very rich in winter.
Hayling Island is over to the right,
across the Emsworth Channel. Continuing southwards will soon bring us to the
Great Deep, a larger stretch of water
which runs across the peninsula. This
stretch of water goes across Thorney
and is a very popular place for birds, in-

Little egret

cluding dabchicks, great crested grebes, egrets, herons and coots.

Just beyond this water is the gate marking the boundary of Minis-
try of Defence land (3), and a telephone here enables you to speak to
the Guard House and have the gate opened to allow entry. Public access to Thorney is only for pedestrians, and the footpath goes all
around the coast. It may be closed occasionally, but it is possible to
telephone 01234 388275 to enquire if access will not be allowed on
any particular day.

Follow the sea wall southwards along the windy western side of
Thorney. The hangars and military buildings can be seen to the left.
The base was used by the RAF from 1935 and taken over by the
Army in 1984.

At the southern end of Thorney are views across the water to East
Head, near the very popular sandy beach at West Wittering, and the
entrance to Chichester Harbour. Protruding from Thorney is Pilsey
Island (4), leased by the MOD to the RSPB as a reserve, and a wonderful place for seeing waders.

Turn to walk northwards, passing the Thorney Island Sailing
Club and Water Sports Centre adjacent to the small church of St
Nicholas. Parts of the church are 800 years old. Just keep going north
along the sea wall to reach the gate at the end of MOD land. Pass the
eastern end of the Great Deep and continue along the embankment.
In addition to the bird life on the shore, there is a grassy wetland area
on the left here, sometimes used by grazing animals but very popular with land birds such as pipits, skylark and crows.

At a stile, which is the end of the MOD land, the coastal path goes

From Thorney Island toward Emsworth

right, and we follow this round to Thornham Marina. If you wish to return quickly to the starting point, it is possible to turn left at this stile, and follow the path, which becomes a driveway, straight out to the main Thorney road. Turn right at the road and after about 200 metres you will reach a footpath to be mentioned later.

The main walk continues along the sea wall and curves round to the marina, crossing a pontoon bridge and then a swing bridge, but really just continuing straight ahead. If it is low tide, the boats will all be resting on the mud, and not looking very exciting, but at high water in summer, boats are moving in or out and it can become quite hectic. Once beyond the boatyard, the path leads on to the South-bourne Scouts Hut where the decision has to be taken (5) – whether to go on for another 8 miles round the Chidham peninsula or to be content with the shorter walk.

Short Cut

To return to the starting point in Emsworth, turn left here, along the driveway leading between the field on the left where dark-bellied brent-geese can sometimes be seen grazing, and the houses on the right. Walk through the iron gates with the name of Thornham Farm written on them. When the driveway splits, with the surfaced road going left, keep straight ahead along the stony track into the farm-yard and pass to the right of the house and through a small gate into an open field. Cross this field, then go over a stile and along a narrow footpath between fences, with an open field on the right. Go over another stile and out on to the road. The shorter route referred to earlier will come up this road from the left.

Go straight across the road, over a stile and through the field to another stile and the chalets on stilts. Turn right here along the stony drive and walk behind the chalets, through the Marina. Retrace your steps to the Slipper Mill and Pool and return into Emsworth and the starting point.

Longer Route

To continue the longer walk, turn right at Southbourne Sea Scouts Hut and keep going eastwards, along the sea wall around the northern edge of the inlet drained by the Thorney Channel. After about a mile of walking in an easterly direction, continue on the sea wall as it turns southwards along the Chidham Peninsula (6). Over to the right will be clear views of the Thorney Island boat yard, across mud or water, depending on the state of the tide.

Walk south along the sea wall for over a mile before veering left, in an easterly direction. This is another stretch where there may be problems if there is a very high spring tide. Along this shore are some remarkable trees which bend down on to the shore but continue growing.

On the mud to the west of Chidham Peninsula is the Nutbourne Marshes Nature Reserve. Just before Cobnor Point is the Warden's hut. Here there is a board containing information about the Nutbourne Marshes and the Stakes. Terns would be noisy here in the summer, but will be thousands of miles away in February. The terns nest on Stake Island, as do small numbers of oyster catchers, redshanks and ringed plovers. In winter there are just the wading birds.

Pass a seat at a convenient location to sit and watch the boats if the tide is in, before continuing north along the path. Detour inland to pass the Cobnor Activity Centre, and then follow the sea wall alongside the Bosham Channel. The coastal path ends opposite Bosham Church and you move away from the sea, passing a magnificent thatched house and then a few other houses, to reach a minor road. Turn right (7) along this road for about 100 metres, and then turn left to follow the signpost to Chidham Church.

Follow this narrow road round past a farm and the Old Rectory to the 13th-century church of St Mary, a plain church, but with many characteristics typical of Sussex churches. A few metres beyond the church is a large flint barn, then a flint farm, and the Old House at Home pub. Continue north for three-quarters of a mile and then turn left, at a footpath sign, along a stony track between two fields. This takes you back to the sea wall.

Turn right (6) along the sea wall and retrace your steps to the Sea Scout Hut. Go through the boat yard to the road, and follow the route described in the short cut to return to Emsworth.

March: Chanctonbury-Cissbury

This downland walk begins near Washington and visits the noted landmark of Chanctonbury Ring and the famous hill fort at Cissbury.

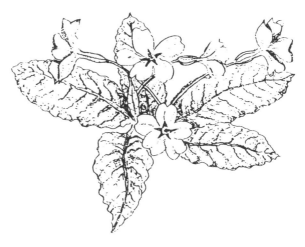

Primrose

Distance: 12 miles with a short cu alternative of 5 miles.

Time: 5 – 6 hours (or 2 – 3 hours).

Terrain: Mostly flat or gently undulating, but does include steep climbs up the escarpment and also up on to the fort at Cissbury. Several places may be very muddy.

Maps: Explorer 121 or Landranger 198.

Starting Point: A small car park (GR 146124) just over a mile along the A283 from Washington to Steyning. Turn right at the cul-de-sac signposted one mile to Chanctonbury, and the car park and picnic site are at the end of this road.

Access: Buses run along the A24 from Worthing to Findon and Washington. There is a railway station in Worthing.

Refreshments: Pubs in Washington and Findon.

Nearest Town: Worthing, where there is a Tourist Information Centre (tel. 01903 210022).

Weather

If it comes in like a lion; it will go out like a lamb, according to the old traditional rhyme, but the truth in this saying is merely the idea that March is a month of remarkable variety. A spell of Arctic or, even worse, Siberian weather is almost inevitable in March, as is a spell of warm, spring-like weather. It is often noticed that all four seasons can be represented sometime during March. The sun is moving north and providing some warmth, but the oceans are still cold, and Siberia is still very cold. Any easterly winds are likely to feel very bitter, and in some localities are referred to as lazy winds because they will go right through you rather than round you.

Dog's mercury

'When the wind is in the east, it brings no good to man nor beast.' There is much truth in this saying, though it applies equally well to January, February or even April.

We traditionally grasp at the first mild spell and pretend that summer is really here, although in reality it is at least two months away at this time. The Meteorological Office, who know about these things, classify March, April and May officially as spring. The 1st of March is the first day of spring and it is time to get out into the countryside to see the reappearance of greenery and hear the ever-increasing noise of birdsong.

The Countryside

The countryside is beginning to change colour as the grass starts its growth, once the temperature stays above 6°C for a few days. The earliest sprouts of green can be seen on trees and in hedgerows too, where honeysuckle and elder are often the first signs of life. On the ground, many of the spurge family will be growing, notably the dog's mercury which provides ground cover in many woods.

Fieldfare

Bird life is becoming more frantic, with early signs of winter flocks beginning to split up, and early nesters already at work gathering suitable material. Rooks will gather at last year's nests, and re-establish pair bonds, which is accompanied by the gathering and presenting of sticks as material with which repair work can begin. The rooks will often sit and chatter at the nests but also have to spend time in the fields searching for food. Many rooks have now developed the habit of searching on the borders of motorways, and they do seem to have a little traffic awareness, and do not wander in front of the cars.

The winter migrants, the fieldfares and redwings, will often gather in large flocks prior to departing, but many will be here until the end of March, when they overlap with the early summer visitors such as chiffchaff and willow warbler arriving from Africa.

On the farms, spraying may have started on the arable fields, some of the dairy cattle may be briefly let out into the fields again, but the main excitement is found in sheep rearing areas, where lambs will be bouncing around and bleating – a real sign of spring.

Chanctonbury Ring

The trees were planted by Charles Goring of Wiston House in 1760, and he used to carry bottles of water up daily to water them when they were tiny seedlings. He planted them when he was a boy and always hoped to live long enough to see them well established. As he did not die until he was 90, his wish was granted. Few of the surviv-

Chanctonbury

ing trees date from 1760, and the ring of trees has become rather thinner since the severe gales of 1987 and the early 1990s. Much recent planting has taken place to restore this small yet prominent clump of woodland. The trees are mostly beech but also include ash, sycamore and some pine. An Iron Age hill fort was located here, with a small enclosure of about 1.4 hectares (3.5 acres). Within the fort is the site of an old Romano-Celtic temple which dates from the 1st century AD. Coins and pottery have been found here. Folklore and legend are attached to this location, including the unlikely story that the devil will appear if you run round the trees seven times.

Cissbury Ring

Cissbury Ring is one of Britain's most impressive prehistoric hill forts. The large bank and ditches enclose about 26 hectares (65 acres), and it is over a mile to walk all the way round – but you should do this, once you have walked up to the triangulation point. It has been estimated that at least 60 000 tons of chalk had to be moved to construct the hill fort. It was an important site, and possibly a regional capital for the Iron Age people. It dates from about 300BC but was abandoned sometime between 50BC and AD50. After that time farming took place on the Ring whilst the Romans were in the area. There is evidence of ploughing in Roman times, and signs of lynchets are visible in the south-eastern part of the fort. The ramparts were rebuilt during the Saxon period.

Downland

Even before the Iron Age inhabitants moved in, there had been a settlement here. At the western end and outside the main ramparts there are hummocks and hollows, the relics of flint workings dating back to 3000BC. Of the 250 pits, several go down vertically to more than 40ft (12 metres), with horizontals radiating outwards. The scale of the mining is rivalled only by that at Grimes Grave in Norfolk. Neolithic men did not use all the sharp flint as many pieces can still be seen lying around. The pits remaining from the mining are now often full of vegetation and create numerous little ecosystems with a special sheltered micro climate for shrubs and small plants to grow. Trees grow in these hollows too, but there are several fine oak and beech actually sitting on the exposed plateau top of the hill.

The Walk

In the car park (1) there is a Countryside Commission board with useful information about the South Downs as a whole and the local area in particular. Opposite the car park is a house with a fine display of snowdrops.

From here, walk up and over the north-facing escarpment of the South Downs, which tower over the car park. From the car park, Great Barn Farm can be seen, one of many farms which have grown up at the foot of the scarp, often where a spring emerging from beneath the chalk provides a reliable water supply. To the left and beyond the farm, Wiston House, now a conference centre, can be seen protruding through the trees.

I last walked here on a mild, windy day in mid-March, reminding myself that it always seems to be windy on the South Downs. From the car park, follow the road towards the Downs. It quickly becomes a track leading into the woods. The final house on the right uses flints as well as bricks and hung tiles, typical of the local Wealden building materials. Pass a small reservoir on the right, and walk along the stony though often muddy track, passing an old quarry, a popular playground in the summer. The track begins to rise and we bend left round the old quarry and climb up into the woods, passing a patch of small box trees. Some of the deciduous trees are beginning to show greenery and dog's mercury covers part of the forest floor, with a few sprouts of cuckoo pint pushing up through the carpet of last year's leaves. The shelter of the woodland will often give a calm and eerie quiet, broken only by the noises of the birds, with tits and finches twittering, green woodpeckers laughing, jays screeching, wrens, blackbirds, song thrushes and robins singing, and pheasants spluttering.

Damaged and broken trees can still be seen in varying stages of decay, mainly relics of strong winds in October 1987 and February 1990, but many new young trees are already growing to replace them. As the old trees rot away, they provide nutrient and create their own little ecosystems while Nature repairs the damage of the storms, coping quite successfully with the meteorological variations and disasters.

Part of the path is sunken, with a higher and drier path alongside, as we climb from 272ft (83 metres) at the car park, to 656ft (200 metres) at the top of the woods (2). This is nearly a mile and is warm work, but the cooler blast may hit us on emerging from the shelter of the trees.

Short Cut

At the major cross-tracks at the top of the woods, turn right along the South Downs Way, a broad and well-worn track, covered by numerous pieces of flint which help to reduce erosion rates along this bridleway. There is likely to be ploughed land to the left with a cereal

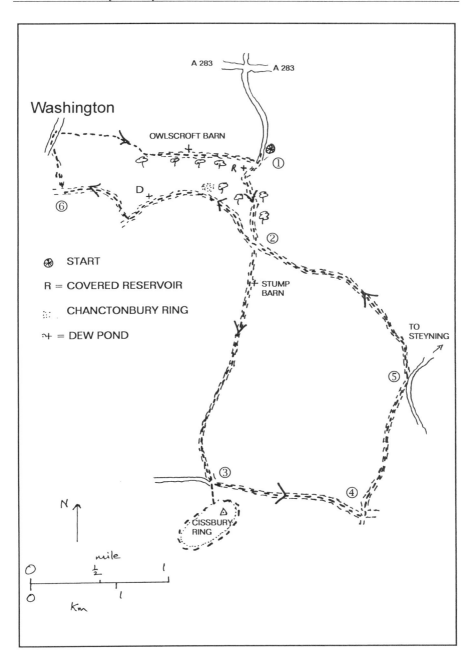

Washington

A 283 A 283

OWLSCROFT BARN

R +

D +

⑥

⑧ START

R = COVERED RESERVOIR

CHANCTONBURY RING

⊹ = DEW POND

①

②

+ STUMP BARN

TO STEYNING

⑤

③

④

N↑

△ CISSBURY RING

mile
½   l

O
O

Km

crop just showing through, and the tops of trees can be seen in Chalkpit Wood to the right, as we walk north-west to the famous clump of trees at Chanctonbury Ring. Pass a cattle grid with a small gate and a stile alongside – ready for all forms of travel – and here is a notice board with a map of the surrounding area. It mentions the fine views, but this can be a very misty and cloudy place on occasions, which may add to the mysterious feeling of the Ring.

Buffeting by strong southerly or south-westerly winds has done serious damage to the Ring. Several young trees are now a few metres in height, some are still protected by tubes and also surrounded by a fence; but they will not receive the same loving care as the original Ring. This clump of trees can be seen for many miles along the South Downs, and can also be seen from several locations on the North Downs over 30 miles away.

Continuing westwards, there is a deep dry valley (Well Bottom) to the left, and a path going off to the right, but we stay on the South Downs Way. This leads just to the south of the triangulation point at 782ft (238 metres), from where there are good views north across the large sandstone quarries to the east of Washington, and an old windmill beyond. In the distance, on a clear day, the North Downs of Surrey may be visible, though there is no outstanding landmark to compare with the reverse view from the North Downs to Chanctonbury.

Past the triangulation point is a dew pond created in 1870, and restored by the Society of Sussex Downsmen in 1970, to commemorate the European Conservation Year. It often holds water, and is a haven for birds. The surrounding area is now classified as an Environmentally Sensitive Area (ESA).

Follow the South Downs Way when it turns right and goes steeply downhill. The path is quite worn here and excellent soil profiles can be seen alongside the path, showing how thin the soil is in this chalkland landscape. Down to the left is Frieslands Farm, located in a delightful, green dry valley, and to the right of the path is an old quarrying area which has been used for scrambling. It contains many small bushes, as well as some grazing areas often used by sheep.

Pass a small gas station, which is a slight blot on the landscape, and just beyond, where a small track comes in from the left, we leave the South Downs Way by turning right (6) at a finger-post. Walk along a narrow footpath between hedges and descend towards Washington, with an old chalk quarry to the left and a field on the right. Go through the woods to reach a stile and possibly a very muddy area where a small stream comes down through the woods. Head diagonally left across a field to a stile and on to a minor road. Turn right and walk for 200 metres before turning right again, off the road, along the path required for the return journey. A further 100 metres along this road is the pub, the Frankland Arms, where good food as well as drink is available if required.

The return walk goes over a stream and then up a short, steep slope where there is a handrail and 26 steps. Emerge to the left side of a large field, probably containing cereals, and walk on, passing a footpath leading off left and then a group of buildings at Tilley's Farm including a large, old, flint barn. Through the hedge to our left can be seen a sandstone quarry, and when the hedge ends, a wooden post with an arrow points to our path. It goes diagonally right across the field towards a gap in the field boundary about 100 metres away. Go through the very thin hedge, and keep straight on across the next field towards the far right corner, at the edge of the woods which clothe the scarp slope up towards Chanctonbury Ring. There are often redwings or fieldfares in this area during the early part of the month, but the changing seasons will be well shown by the fact that a few of the little green warblers, willow warbler or chiffchaff may be heard singing here by the end of the month.

At the foot of the wooded scarp, the path turns left along the margin of the woods, with the field to the left. Primroses are numerous around this area. Go through a gate with a notice about the presence of cattle and there is a grassy area to the right. This leads up to the Ring. Walk on past Owlscroft Barn and its adjacent flint-faced ruin, through another old, iron gate, and along the field margins to return to the starting point. This is often a muddy area – as indeed are many places in the countryside at this time of year. This is especially so here, with clay soils and also water emerging from the bottom of the chalk hills on the right – an important reason for the location of farms and, sometimes, villages at the foot of the escarpment.

Longer Route

Having emerged from the woods on the scarp, go straight across the South Downs Way and head southwards. The track leads across an open landscape, sloping gently down along a ridge. The fields are very stony with pieces of flint, and if planted will just be showing the young, green shoots. Pass the old and partially ruined Stump Barn.

Still descending slightly, a line of trees and shrubs on the right will provide some shelter from the wind on this bracing and exposed down, and in the midst of the Scots pine and hawthorn may be some gorse in flower to add a little brightness to the scene. An uprooted Scots pine will indicate how exposed this location really is.

A few birds survive in these trees, a robin or great tit may be singing, and a yellowhammer is likely to be in evidence, wearing his bright summer colouring. Squirrels live in the small wood on the left-hand side. Finches are probably still in their winter flocks, but lapwings will be starting to settle in for their nesting season, and they may show off with a display of aerobatics. Skylarks will be singing. They may now have split up from their winter flocks and be pairing off for breeding. Gulls are likely to be flying around overhead. Rooks and jackdaws live in the area, too, though the jackdaws are not as common as they were in the days of Richard Jefferies. He told many stories of these birds in his 19th-century writing on the Downlands.

At a cross-tracks keep straight ahead, with a compass bearing of about 200, and after a quarter of a mile go straight over the next cross-tracks, passing a small woodland area. The impressive sight of Cissbury Ring is beginning to dominate the views ahead as we squelch along a very muddy track. Horses and Land Rovers contribute to the wear and tear along this track. The path is following a ridge, and away to both left and right the land can be seen sloping down into dry valleys, with Findon and the A24 to the right, but miles of rolling downland to the left.

Suddenly a small car park is reached (3), and it is unlikely to be empty. It will not be crowded with walkers and picnickers at this time of the year, but there will be the dog walkers from nearby Findon and elsewhere. Paths circle all round the circumference of this hill fort, but we can go straight up. Cissbury Ring is owned by the National Trust and there is an excellent information board at the foot of the steep slope. Here we can learn some of the history and natural history of the area. The embankments around this fort are at a height of 492ft (150 metres) above sea level in the south-western

corner, and 574ft (175 metres) in the southeast. The triangulation point on top is at 603ft (184 metres).

Go straight on up the steep slope, even though it may be slippery with the clingy mud found on chalklands after rainy weather. It is amazing how the chalk which is so porous can create such a slippery surface after recent rain. At the top, around the triangulation point, notice the fine grassy cover, although the thin soil has often been removed to reveal the underlying chalk. Many places on the slopes have been covered with netting or wire mesh in order to try to hold the slopes together, and prevent erosion. The delightful springy and green turf is a natural type of vegetation, remaining in this area because it has not been ploughed in recent years, unlike so much of the Downs. Sheep grazing the land help to control larger plants and enable the smaller plants to survive. Without the sheep to nibble them away, larger plants and small trees would grow and dominate the vegetation, thereby preventing some of the grasses from surviving.

In addition to the grasses there are many flowering plants, including eight species of orchid. Other small flowers occur and one unusual variety is the field fleawort, which was used by the Iron Age people to discourage lice in their bedding. In the summer, butterflies are numerous, with a total of 28 varieties including the rare Adonis blue. There is also a rich bird life, with noisy skylarks being particularly busy with their singing in March. Green woodpeckers, pipits, kestrels and many others can be seen in March, but there is unlikely to be any sign of the adders, slow-worms and lizards which will appear in the warmer weather.

The views all round are magnificent, with the coast to the south and the cliffs of the Isle of Wight being visible on a clear day. To the east, the line of the South Downs can be seen going on beyond the Shoreham cement works and its feeder quarry to Beachy Head.

There are greener views looking north along the main line of the walk, although some fields are likely to be brown from ploughing or even quite light where the chalky soil is showing through.

As we complete the circuit back to the small car park, notice our arrival path stretching away up the dip slope towards Chanctonbury Ring on the skyline – one of the most, if not the most, distinctive landscapes of the Downs.

For the return walk, go through the gate near the car park and turn right (eastwards) to follow a stony track passing to the left of a large barn. After a downhill stretch of about a mile, the path divides and we take the left fork. Pass a magnificent dry valley to the left, and climb steadily up to a crossing point of paths and bridleways (4). Turn left along a bridleway which has a downhill slope at first, and then a long, steady climb to a minor road where there is a small parking area (5).

The path ahead does not go on to the road but veers away to the left, having been joined by the South Downs Way, which comes across the road at this point. The open view to the east looks above the deep hollow of the Steyning Bowl, towards the Shoreham Cement works.

Follow the South Downs Way, passing the flint memorial to Walter Langmead, a Sussex farmer, near a cross-paths, and keeping straight on towards Chanctonbury Ring. Pass the triangulation point (620ft, 189 metres) to the left, but just keep going for a mile to reach the cross-paths at the top of Chalk Pit Wood (2). Do not turn right into the woods to descend to the starting point, but keep ahead and follow the walk already described above in the short cut route.

April: Petworth

This walk passes through Petworth Park, the small town of Petworth and neighbouring farmland, passing the Coultershaw Mill and River Rother on the way.

Great Crested Grebe

Distance: 7 miles, or 8 miles if walking round the western edge of Petworth Park.

Time: 3 – 4 hours, though extra time may be spent in Petworth town or visiting Petworth House.

Terrain: Gently undulating, and muddy in places. There are several stiles, though none in the park. It is all gentle walking.

Maps: Explorers 133 and 121, or Landranger 197.

Starting Point: The National Trust car park alongside the A238, one mile north of Petworth. GR 966238.

Access: Regular bus services run to Petworth from Midhurst and from Guildford.

Refreshments: Available in Petworth and at the pub in Coultershaw.

Nearest Town: Petworth, where there is a Tourist Information Centre (tel. 01798 343523).

Weather

The mixed bag of weather during the month will often include the famed April showers, which are associated with airstreams following on behind Atlantic depressions. These airstreams come from the west or north-west, and bring quick-moving showers followed by bright spells of sunshine. The ocean is at its coldest in March and April, and air blowing from the sea may be quite stable, though still able to produce showers rather than prolonged spells of rain. Early days of the cricket season are often interrupted by these outbursts. The showers will generally be of rain, but hail or sleet also occur. Snow may still fall in the Highlands, but is unlikely in Sussex, which is now warming up with the increasing height of the midday sun. The first really warm days of the year are likely to occur during the month.

'April weather; both rain and sunshine together.' This old weather saying gives a good indication of the month's conditions. Another saying with some validity is the old French opinion that, 'It is not April without a frosty crown.' An occasional frost is certainly likely to occur during the month.

The Countryside

Longer hours of daylight and warmer temperatures have contributed to the real beginning of spring growth. The grass will be growing, as average daily temperatures are above 6°C, and the wild flowers will be making the countryside much more colourful. Spring flowers will bloom whatever the weather conditions have been. Dairy cattle will be back out in the fields after a winter spent indoors, and summer visiting birds will be arriving from Africa. Earliest arrivals include the tiny, green warblers – the chiffchaff and willow warbler. These can be heard singing and can still be seen in trees which are only just showing their first touches of green. Hawthorn hedges will be sprouting and many trees will be showing increasing amounts of green during the month, with many being fully in leaf by the end of the month. Beech trees, as well as the numerous beech hedges, are often quite late in growing their leaves, with leaf growth continuing well into May.

The old saying,

> *'Ash before oak, look for a soak;*
> *Oak before ash, look for a splash,'*

may be a pessimistic thought that it is going to be wet anyway, but in recent years the ash seems to have been generally later than the oak, whatever the spring weather.

The old saying originated because it was traditionally thought that if the oak were in leaf before the ash, a fine and productive year would follow; but if the ash were in leaf first, the summer would be cool. Records kept in the 19th century showed many years when the oak was in leaf first, summers were good and harvests above average; the reverse being seen to be true when the ash was first to be in leaf. A few years were noted when the trees burst into leaf at about the same time, and the harvests were average.

Many of the resident birds will be nest building and can be seen carrying twigs or grass to their nesting sites. Rooks and magpies are birds which can often be seen struggling with sticks longer than themselves, whilst blackbirds carry beaks full of grass, and very cleverly can pick up more grass without dropping what they already have in their beak. Most of the work is done by the female, though the male will occasionally bring some material, or will help by singing to entertain his mate and also defend their territory from rival birds.

Petworth Park

Petworth Park covers an area of 299 hectares (738 acres) and has been managed by the National Trust since 1947. It was landscaped by Capability Brown, who drew up his plans in 1752. Although he made minor changes in the gardens, his main work was in the park, where he created a lake and planted many groups of trees. The park is now fully mature with clumps of trees and fine vistas – often enhanced by the presence of a herd of deer.

The Pleasure Gardens

The Petworth House garden dates from about 1600 and was adjusted several times in later centuries, though the original design was never totally replaced. Amongst Capability Brown's changes were the creation of the ha-ha around the garden to keep out the deer, and the planting of the sweet chestnut, plane and lime trees. In the garden there is a wide variety of trees, but the bright yellow of daffodils will be showing in several open spaces. Other wild flowers include primroses and violets, and there are also tulips and grape hyacinths, growing in grass areas in the midst of the trees, shrubs and buildings. Prominently located in the gardens are the Rotunda with its ten Ionic columns, and the Roman Doric Temple. The temple contains a memorial plaque to Henry Scawen Wyndham, a lieutenant in the 9th Lancers, who died at El Alemein on October 28th 1942. From the highest point of the garden are magnificent views across the park.

Petworth House

The 17th-century house, also in the care of the National Trust, is open to visitors from the end of March till the beginning of November, daily except for Thursday and Friday (but open on Good Friday). The house contains paintings by Van Dyck, Reynolds and Blake, and there is a special Turner room for a collection of his works. There is also a magnificent state room with carvings and furniture by Grinling Gibbons.

Petworth Manor was given to Queen Adeliza by her husband, Henry I, and she gave it to her brother, who took the name of Percy when he married into that famous northern family. The descendants of the Percy family have been living here ever since, and portraits of many of the ancestors can be seen in the house. The house was rebuilt between 1688 and 1696 by the Duke of Somerset, who had married a Percy heiress.

The west front of Petworth House and part of the formal garden, c1700

The Wyndham family, related to the Percys, took over Petworth in the 18th century, and also acquired the title of Earl of Egremont. It was the second Earl of Egremont who employed Capability Brown to landscape the park, and it was the art-loving third Earl of Egremont who collected a few Turner paintings, and then supported this artist and his work. J.M.W. Turner (1775-1851) became a friend and a regular visitor to Petworth, and he painted many scenes in the park showing the work of Capability Brown.

This house has one of the few real tennis courts in the world. The game has been played here since the 16th century, though the present court only dates from 1872.

Petworth Dolls' Museum

The museum is open from March to October, on Thursdays to Sundays, from 10.30am to 5pm. This museum contains a variety of houses, including several modern dolls' houses on a one twelfth scale.

Coultershaw Beam Pump

This pump, dating from about 1790, was built to supply extra water to Petworth House, and was able to pump 23 000 gallons per day from the river up to Petworth. It is now a scheduled ancient monument, and is occasionally open to the public (first and third Sundays in April to September, from 11am till 5pm). It was restored by the Sussex Industrial Archaeology Society and restarted in 1980, by Lord Egremont. The building housing the pump also contains a few smaller water pumps, many in working order, as well as a history of the local area and the Rother navigation.

The Walk

From the car park (1), walk past the information board and downhill towards the small lake called Lower Pond. There are trees and the road to our left, and the park extending away to the right. The trees on the left will probably contain many thrushes and blackbirds, robins, twittering tits and finches, nuthatches, and one or two early summer visitors. Notice that many of the young trees are surrounded by a protective fence to keep the deer away. Pass to the left of a circular patch of trees before reaching the lake, Lower Pond. Bird life on the lake is likely to include Canada geese, mallard, coots,

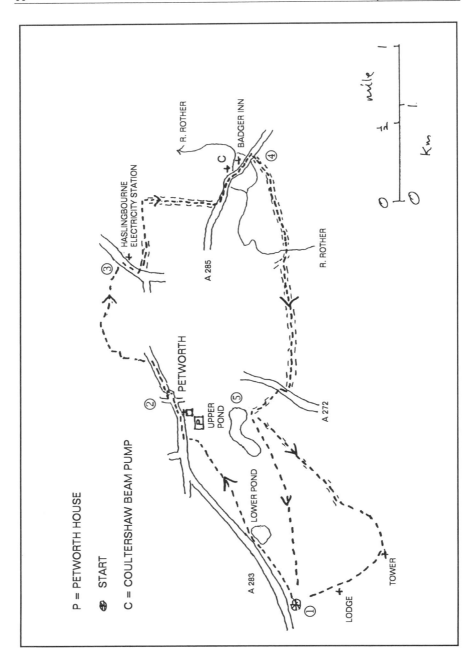

moorhens, great crested grebes, and possibly cormorants. The entire park is rich in wild life, with a large herd of deer as well as a variety of birds. Most numerous and noisy among the latter are likely to be the green woodpeckers, which will probably be heard calling, and seen flying away, with their unusual, undulating style of flight. Jackdaws are also numerous and noisy, as they chack chack chack all day long.

Pass to the left of the lake and keep ahead, passing to the left of two clumps of trees. Then bear right and climb the hill, heading towards the right-hand end of the wall which is straight ahead. The wall is the boundary of the Pleasure Gardens, designed originally by the 9th Earl of Northumberland (the Percy family) about 1600, and now open to visitors at the same times as Petworth House.

Walk on a level stretch with the walled garden to our left, and a ha-ha ditch between the park and the wall. Keep straight ahead and drop down towards the house. Unless you intend to visit the house now, leave the park before reaching the house by going left at the iron gate and beneath the tunnel. At the gate is the notice, 'The gate is open from 8am – 9pm, or dusk if earlier. Please keep dogs on the lead to avoid disturbing the deer and the sheep.'

Walk through the Cow Yard, past the workshops and out on to the road – what a contrast this provides. This is the busy A283 so take care. For many years there have been plans and discussions about providing Petworth with a bypass, which it desperately needs, but no suitable location has yet been agreed upon.

Cross over and turn right, passing Preyste House and Monk House on the left, and then the 14th-century church of St Mary the Virgin on the right. The church is of stone, with a brick tower, and was largely rebuilt about 1827. Sir Charles Berry designed the tower and spire in 1827, but the spire was removed in 1947.

Walk along East Street with its antique shops, and at the crossroads (2) our way ahead is straight on along Middle Street. Before doing this, it may be of interest to turn right to walk into the Market Square, the centre of Petworth, just a few metres away, where there are many fine buildings.

The Town Hall (Leconfield Hall) in the Market Square was built by the Earl of Egremont in 1793, but has been much restored. On the north wall is a bust of William III, a copy of the bust to be found in Petworth House. Around the square are some of Petworth's narrow

streets, with a few very old houses, narrow alleyways and court-
yards. A cobbled road (Lombard Street) leads up to the church, and
there are shops and cafés and pubs if required, and a Dolls' Museum.

Return to Middle Street and walk along it to High Street, then
turn left at the curved Corner Cottage. Middle Street, High Street,
and its continuation, Grove Street, contain a variety of interesting,
old houses,.including buildings of stone and with hung tiles. Many
of the houses were provided for the workers on the Leconfield (the
Petworth Park) Estate. The small Petworth Cottage Museum at
number 346 High Street is open from April to October in the afternoons. It provides an opportunity to see a 17th-century worker's cottage restored to how it looked about 1910.

At the end of
the houses, we
turn left between
the allotments
and walk out to a
patch of grass,
where a seat might
provide a good
spot for a picnic.
Lawn   tennis
courts are on the
left and the open
grassland on the
right, with a few
trees and clumps
of daffodils. There
are   primroses
around here, too,
and the hawthorn
hedges will just be
turning green.

The path leads
through to a stile
where we turn
right. Walk to an-
other stile and out
into an open field.

April sunshine in Petworth

The grassy track heads slightly down the side of a steep, little valley to a gate, then through a few trees to an open field and a finger-post. Bear right along the lower edge of the slope, and follow a line of oak trees to two stiles with a fairly new footbridge in between. This is Byworth Bridge and was built in 1996. Alongside the river here are many wild flowers: celandines, wood anemones and even a few bluebells may be in flower before the end of the month. The river is now to the right as we continue through the next field, over a stile and across a patch of rough ground with interesting bird and plant life. Go over another stile and through the next field, where ladies smock grows alongside the stream to the right. Negotiate another stile to emerge on a road near Haslingbourne Electricity Station (3).

Turn right to pass Haslingbourne House and the river, before turning left on the public footpath which follows a surfaced track. This leads to the right side of houses and then over a stile and straight across two fields. Good views of the South Down scarp near Duncton Down and Bignor Hill can be seen ahead. At the track, a right turn leads us out to the A285.

At the road, turn left into Coultershaw, where the River Rother is bridged across three channels. The old mill race is at the first bridge, on the northern branch of the river, and adjacent to it is the large barn housing the Coultershaw Beam Pump.

Walk on past the Badger Inn, originally built as the Railway Hotel. To the left of the main road bridge is the old, two-arched bridge, beyond which is the old railway station, now a private house. Along the main road, just a few metres past the river, turn right (4) along a track, to pass two small cottages on the right and then Kilsham Farm on the left. Cross over the River Rother at the footbridge, to reach Rotherbridge Farm in its picturesque setting. Keep straight ahead for about 50 metres, and where the track begins to bend right, fork left on a narrow, gullied track. This leads between bare rock walls, up to 5m high, and is the line of the old turnpike road from Chichester to Petworth. There was originally a road bridge over the Rother, but it was dismantled when road traffic ceased, which is why there is now only a footbridge. Follow the track, which was the main road until the road through Coultershaw was opened about 1800, and note the rich growth of flowers in this sheltered lane and the overhanging trees making an archway. This track is Hungers Lane and it leads us through to the main A272.

Turn right, then cross over at the gates to walk into Petworth Park between the lodge houses. Follow the stony track as it bends round to the right, approaching the lake, Upper Pond. Fork right if visiting the house, or along the left side of Upper Pond if returning to the starting point. The lake is home to an interesting assortment of bird life, including gulls, coots, moorhens, ducks and geese, and honking and quacking noises will be heard – especially if you have any remnants of your picnic to feed to them (5).

For the shorter alternative, just continue along the side of the lake. Beyond the end of the lake, keep straight ahead along a shallow valley. Once beyond the higher ground, the water of Lower Pond will come into sight over to the right. Keep left of this lake and head over to the far right corner of the park to return to the starting point. Look out for the fallow deer and the bird life as you cross the park.

The longer alternative will add a mile to the total distance, but will show more of the park and give better and longer views round the countryside. For this, follow the stony drive – a continuation of the route walked into the park from the lodge houses. This drive bends away from the lake and climbs steadily towards the western margin of the park. Over to the left can be seen the buildings of Tillington village. There are often deer up on this higher plateau, and some of the supplementary feed they have during the winter may still be lying around. As the path gets higher the views improve, both across the park and eastwards over the Weald.

The track drops a little and up a dry valley to the left can be seen some of the buildings of Upperton village. At the next dry valley, leave the surfaced track and climb steeply up past a bench, from which there are wonderful views across the Weald, to visit the small tower house on the margin of the park. This turreted tower is adjacent to a small, covered reservoir, and is close to the wall surrounding the entire park. A minor road is just on the other side of this wall.

From the tower, return to the starting point of the walk by passing through a group of tall beech trees. Walk parallel to the wall towards a clump of pine trees, and as the wall bends left, we descend towards a small house on the park margin. Keep straight ahead back to the car park.

May: Alfriston

The main walk goes east on clear paths from Alfriston to pass over the Downs and in a circuit via Wilmington. The extension walk, if required, goes west to Alfriston and back along the top of the Downs.

Distance: 9 miles, with an extension of 5½ miles

Time: 4 – 5 hours (or 7 hours)

Terrain: Undulating, with two fairly steep climbs up on to the top of the Downs. Many stiles will be encountered.

Maps: Explorer 123 or Landrangers 198 and 199.

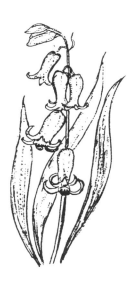

Bluebell

Starting Point: At the car park in Alfriston, GR 523033. Alfriston is located between Newhaven and Eastbourne, and can be reached along the B2108, which links the A27 with the coastal road the A259. There is ample parking space in the village.

Access: Buses run to Alfriston from Seaford and Eastbourne.

Refreshments: Cafés, pubs and hotels in Alfriston.

Nearest Towns: Seaford, which has a Tourist Information Centre (01323 897426), and Eastbourne.

Weather

Depressions are still likely to be passing over from the west, bringing rainy and unsettled weather, but high pressure from Europe or the Arctic can prevent this movement. Cold weather can still occur, and although unusual, snow showers have occasionally been experienced, and frosty nights are often recorded.

Whereas high pressure from the north or east can bring cool temperatures because the North Sea is still cold, high pressure from the south will give daily temperatures of 20°C or more. These hot days can occur at any time, but are more likely towards the end of the month when there is often a spell of settled weather. This is brought by the Azores High Pressure system. This permanently affects the Sahara, but in summer it moves north to give the Mediterranean lands their long, hot summers, and occasionally can reach far enough north to affect the British Isles, especially Sussex and the south-east of England.

'Ne'er cast a clout till May is out,' is sound advice if cold northerly or easterly winds are blowing, though whether May means the month or the may flower, a country name for the hawthorn blossom, is less certain. It received the name of 'may' because it was noticed that the flowers came out on the first of May, under the old Julian calendar. When the calendar was changed by 11 days in 1752, the 1st became the 12th, and so in most years the hawthorn now flowers in the middle of the month.

The Countryside

Though cold easterlies from Siberia can still blow and sharp frosts occasionally occur, to the dismay of fruit growers, May does contain some glorious days. By the end of the month the countryside is at its greenest, and it is truly a 'green and pleasant land' (William Blake). All the new plants are in leaf, and it is too soon for dry spells to be turning anything yellow and parched. The only yellow colour comes from the numerous flowers which are at their best, and fields of rape which are at their most colourful. These plants can also give off a smell, which is less attractive than their appearance.

Wild flowers, fruits and berries add variety to the colour of the countryside. Hedges, verges and banks are covered with grasses, which grow tall during the month, and the many coloured flowers which grow in their midst. There are even a few places where bright red poppies can be seen on field margins, where farmers have not used herbicide to kill the weeds which would otherwise grow in the crops and reduce the yields. Farmers have been positively encouraged to allow wild flowers to grow along the field margins as they will encourage insects, which will then enable birds to nest and find adequate food for their young. Butterflies can also have more chance of breeding if there are food plants available for their caterpillars.

The children's song which refers to 'gathering nuts in May, on a cold and frosty morning' seems not to make sense as there are no nuts to be found in May. However, 'nuts' here is a corruption of knots or sprigs of may. The song does quite accurately suggest that in May, the mornings can be cool.

The Clergy House

This 14th-century, timber-framed house was the first building to be purchased by the National Trust – for £10 in 1896. It was falling into disrepair until saved by the Trust. Although called the Clergy House, it was not necessarily the residence of the clergy, but was owned by the Church. For many years the vicar tried to maintain the property but it had become too difficult and too expensive by the 1890s, which is why it was offered to the National Trust. It is open daily from the end of March until the end of October, except on Tuesdays and Fridays.

Coombes and terracettes

During the time of the last ice advance, much of southern England experienced tundra climate similar to that experienced in northern Canada today. Frosts were common and repeated freezing and thawing of water particles in the soil and rock loosened the surface layers. These would slide downhill to form the small ledges known as terracettes on the hillside. In several places so much soil and rock slithered away down the hillside that large hollows called coombes were formed – and good examples will be noticed on this walk.

Long Man of Wilmington

A late 18th-century manuscript is the first known reference to the Long Man, but this mysterious figure on the hillside was probably covered by vegetation and therefore not often noticed until cleared in 1873. It is now cared for by the Sussex Archaeological Society, who marked out the figure in concrete blocks in 1969. Formerly just a marking in the grass, the Long Man is 230ft high (70 metres). The true shape of the Long Man as seen from the air is rather elongated, so that it looks correctly proportioned when seen from the valley. To the right of the man is an old chalk pit, dating from 1750 to 1850, and there are flint mines to the left which date from the New Stone Age, about 3500BC.

Wilmington Church

The church of St Mary and St Peter has a small, squat tower with a weatherboard and shingle turret. Above the porch is a room called the Prior's Chapel. Parts of the chancel date from the 12th century and much of the nave dates from the 14th. In the 13th-century North Chapel, now used as the vestry, is the colourful Bee and Butterfly window, with ten species of insect grouped round the central panel. (They are Camberwell Beauty, scarlet tiger moth, large copper, emperor moth, hawkmoth, wall butterfly, small tortoiseshell, large tortoiseshell, Apollo butterfly, and humble bee.) On the north side of the church stands the amazing old yew, with a girth of 23ft (7 metres) and an age probably greater than that of the church.

Berwick Church

Part of this church dates from the 12th century, though much was restored in the 1850s. The church is most noted for its wall paintings, commissioned by the Bishop of Chichester, and painted in 1942 and 43, by Vanessa Bell, Quentin Bell and Duncan Grant. The church has been unlucky with damage: it was hit by a flying bomb during the Second World War, struck by lightning in 1982 and damaged by the powerful gale of October 1987, when the church spire was slightly bent. It is a beautiful, small church with a shingle spire, and is surrounded by a colourful churchyard.

Berwick Church

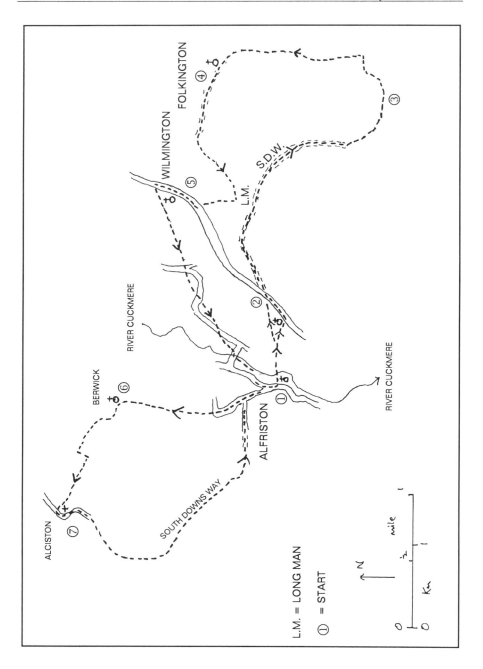

FOLKINGTON

WILMINGTON

④

③

S.D.W.

L.M.

⑤

RIVER CUCKMERE

②

RIVER CUCKMERE

BERWICK

⑥

①

ALFRISTON

ALCISTON

⑦

SOUTH DOWNS WAY

L.M. = LONG MAN

① = START

N

Km

mile

0

0

The Walk

Start by going along the main street (1) and past the old cross. Just beyond the George Inn, take the narrow lane (locally called a twitten) which leads down to the Tye, the village green area in front of the church. Both the church and the Old Clergy House on the far side of the green are worth close inspection. It is a beautiful and well kept village, a past winner of the best-kept small village in East Sussex, with many interesting and immaculate buildings,. Much use is made of flint as a building material.

Our route continues from the twitten along the walled path to the White Bridge over the River Cuckmere. This important footbridge was rencvated in 1984 and from it you will see great views already opening up ahead, so press on, without waiting to feed the ducks. Cross over the narrow road, to the right of Plonk Barn, built of local materials in 1698, and restored magnificently in 1985. Follow the path at the side of the converted barn and after 150 metres, where it splits, you have a choice. Either take the left turn through the hedge and then go diagonally to the right and gently uphill through two fields to a small, stony car park, or go straight on if interested in seeing Lullington Church. The path to Lullington is straight ahead alongside the hedge, then into a small wood and along a surfaced path. The church is to the left. For the onward route we go out on to the road and turn left, to walk about 400 metres to the small, stony car park where the alternative route also leads. Lullington Church is one of the smallest churches in England, but is only the chancel of a larger medieval church. It is a flint church with some hung tiles and a small weatherboard belfry.

Cross the road (2) and walk on the bridleway which is the South Downs Way. On a sunny day the white chalk may prove dazzling, as will some of the views in this near perfect, rural environment. Skylarks will be singing noisily, and in the dry valley to the right there may be cows peacefully grazing. Cowslips will still be in flower where the track begins to bend round the head of the dry valley.

The main track continues to bend right, but go straight ahead by the fence on the left to see the Long Man of Wilmington. The origins of this figure cut in the chalk are quite obscure, though almost certainly he is prehistoric. We are really going straight on along the South Downs Way, but just climb over the high stile to have a look at him from above. We can see the dew pond beneath his feet. After climbing the stile, go away from the fence, diagonally up to the top of Windover Hill. Does this springy turf resemble the original natural vegetation? Rabbits certainly enjoy it, as there is plenty of evidence of their existence. They help to preserve the grassland by nibbling away at any plant which tries to grow too tall, and in this way help to preserve a rich variety of tiny grasses and flowering plants. At the top are New Stone Age mounds dating from about 3500BC, evidence of Bronze Age inhabitants from about 1000BC and old chalk pits.

On the top, join the main path again and turn left to continue along the South Downs Way. At the gate the path splits, and we fork right and round the head of another dry valley. Narrower than the previous valley, it has the curves of a clear meander where the river must have been flowing when the water was on the surface. Hawthorn, blackthorn, gorse, and wayfaring trees clothe the slopes. The wayfaring tree (viburnum lantana) and its white flowers are very common in this area, and it will be in flower until July. A kestrel is likely to be patrolling, hoping to find a mouse, a shrew, or even a grasshopper.

The path splits again where the fence bends, and we take the left fork this time, across a grassy track towards a marker post. We are still on the turf so it's pleasant for walking, with a cropped field to the left, and the usual supply of skylarks singing noisily. Once past the shell of the stone barn and an old chalk pit on the left, we reach a gate where many more bluebells are growing. Woodland, the sea and open downland can all be seen in a panoramic view.

Go through the gate and along a grassy patch between a field and woods to another gate. Keep straight on, but soon turn left to go downhill through the woods along a stony track. Blackcaps, robins and many other birds will be singing lustily, the pheasants may be calling and the scent of wild garlic may be strong. At the bottom, the path splits and the South Downs Way leads off to the right, but we leave it here and fork left (3). There is a good view into the dry valley called Hayward's Bottom on the left.

Pass through a dense shrubbery of small trees, rich in bluebells, bird life, squirrels and butterflies. The colour of red campion and the song of willow warblers was particularly prominent when I last walked this way. At a meeting point with a track, turn right. Soon turn sharp left, more than a right angle, along a narrow track between hedges. This can be muddy even in dry weather because of horses, and here, as on earlier paths, a narrow gorge has been formed by water erosion in many stretches in the middle of this path.

We are now turning away from Jevington, which we never quite reached though it was visible through the trees, and heading towards Wilmington. The thick hedges are full of wild flowers and bird life, including goldfinches, hedge sparrows and many other small birds, which can now keep themselves hidden as the greenery increases their cover.

This small bird paradise is part of the Wealdway long-distance path, which we follow towards Wilmington. Just after a path leads off to the right, but before a flint house on the right, a narrow path goes diagonally up to the left, and this is our route. Some steps take us down and then up across a narrow gully. We then go over a stile and diagonally across a field to a marker post. Now out in the open landscape again, there are views ahead and a small hill, Middle Brow, up to the left. Behind and to the right, you can see Polegate, Eastbourne and the continuing line of the South Downs as they reach their easterly extremity.

Cross the next field to a stile. On the left is the impressive line of the north-facing scarp, heavily scalloped by coombes in which there are many small ledges along the slopes, possibly the result of solifluction.

Go on diagonally down the steep slope of a dry valley, treading on some of the terracettes, using them as steps, and reach the corner of the narrow field. Go over the stile and across a cropped field to the far right corner. Here we rejoin the hedged track we were on a few minutes ago, before cutting off a corner – perhaps keen birdwatchers should stay on the track?

Notice the small patches of woodland, looking light green and feathery, at the foot of the coombes. Near Folkington Church the path splits, but we keep straight ahead (4), on the right margin of the woodland, and enter Folkington Estate. (Ignore the Private Property notice, but be sure to stay on the public right of way). A few metres along the road leading off to the right is St Peter's Church, with a flint nave and chancel. The bell turret is weatherboarded.

Our path leads on to Wilmington, passing a large number of fallen trees from the storms of recent years. There are good views to the right, across the Weald, probably with yellow fields of rape providing the brightest colour. Continue along the track, with a small wood on the left, but when the track goes down to the right, keep straight ahead along a level path and walk towards the foot of the steep slope. Sitting on this slope, before reaching the huge figure of the Long Man, I was surrounded by primroses and violets and could hear the rooks cawing in the rookery near to Wilmington Church. Skylarks, yellowhammers, willow warblers and blackbirds were singing in the bushes around me and, as might have happened a hundred years ago when they were much more numerous, jackdaws were searching for food.

At the foot of the Long Man, now fenced off to protect him from wear and tear, and just before reaching the dew pond, we turn right through a small gate to walk along the narrow path between fields. The Arlington Reservoir can be seen two miles away to the north. At the road turn right and walk into the village of Wilmington (5). An information board in the car park mentions the obscurity of the Long Man's origins.

Continue along the road, passing the converted barn on the left (the granite memorial seat looking out of place in this flinty territory) and the pound in which stray animals used to be secured, before reaching the old priory. These remains of a Benedictine priory date from the 13th century. In the surviving buildings there is now an agricultural museum with a large collection of old items relating to farm life in former centuries. It was clearly much harder in those days. Just past the priory is the church of St Mary and St Peter, which was built to serve the monks in the priory as well as the parishioners, and was connected to the priory by a covered cloister.

To walk back to Alfriston, leave the church and turn left along the village street. Opposite Stable Cottage, which is on the right, is a small footpath going left between two houses. Follow the concrete path between two gardens then left along a driveway behind the rookery and the church. Opposite a small gate leading out of the churchyard, and before the house at the end of the drive, we turn right to go across this field. The path bends left in a dog-leg, giving views back to the church and priory and across to the Long Man. Pass through a hedge and straight on along a broad, grassy track in a cropped field.

Turn left at the road, pass Milton Street Farm and then go right at the telephone box, following the signpost to Alfriston. Cross two fields then a small road, and continue straight across the middle of another field. At the next road turn left, pass the fine buildings of Milton Court Farm, with its old flint wall as well as some modern barns, and then turn right to Alfriston. Cross the fields to the road and Long Bridge, and from here walk down either side of the River Cuckmere for the final few hundred metres. This river is still tidal, and is well embanked for flood prevention. Ducks and swans may accompany us on this final stretch of the walk.

The Star Inn

Back in Alfriston, do visit the cruciform parish church of St Andrew and the Clergy House, and you may be tempted by the pubs or cafés or shops. The Star Inn is one of England's oldest inns, part of it dating from the 13th century, and during the 16th century it was known as the Star of Bethlehem. There has been a village on this site since prehistoric times. The market grew here because of the River Cuckmere and the routes along the Downs. The ancient cross in the centre is one of only two left in Sussex (the other is in Chichester). The old cottages on the main street used to house tradesmen, but now retain merely the names e.g. Saddler's Cottage, Weaver's Cottage. The Wingrove Inn and adjacent cottages used to be the famous Wingrove Racing Stables. Twytten House is now an antique shop but was formerly connected with boat building. Alfriston was a small port when the River Cuckmere was larger and had not been restricted within its embankments, and smuggling was an important part of life.

Extension Walk

If it is a nice day and you still feel like more walking, once you have had refreshment and a good look round the village, another excellent walk can be had by walking westwards from Alfriston for a further distance of 5½ miles.

Depart from the Market Cross (1) and walk along the road, past the other, smaller short-term car park, to reach the end of the houses, and begin to climb slightly. Where the narrow road (Winton Street) turns sharp right, go straight ahead along the stony track towards Comp Barn on the skyline, an immaculately restored, old flint building. After about 50 metres, as the track bends left and begins to descend, go right over a stile and then straight ahead along the field margin. Keep straight ahead for four fields and this leads straight towards the church at Berwick (6). At the track just before the church, turn left, but detour after a few metres to visit the church of St Michael and All Angels.

We continue the walk by turning left out of the churchyard, to retrace steps along the lane to the track we were on earlier. Turn right at the track and follow it as it leads along an open field, with a hedge, wooden summer house and fine house to the right. At the end of the field turn right along a concrete track, which soon begins to bend right. However, we turn left to pass between two houses on the right and a barn and farmyard on the left. Keep straight on past these buildings and go out along a clear path into the middle of open fields, with great views to the South Downs scarp on our left, but not such good views of the A27, a few hundred metres to the right.

Walk straight through the fields. When you reach a hedge and stile, turn left to walk towards the Downs for 150 metres then turn right for another straight walk along field margins towards the church at Alciston. At the end of the open fields, go straight on, over a stile, with the stone wall of the churchyard on the left, and through a gate. Turn left here to visit the church before following the path to the right which leads out to the road (7).

The flint church is of Norman origin but was restored in 1853. It is simple and light, with no chancel arch and exposed beams in the roof of the nave. The church is part of a magnificent complex of old buildings, including the farm next door and a clergy house.

Walk out to the road and turn left, where remains of the 14th-century dovecote can be seen. Pass Court House Farm – its enormous, old tithe barn is 170ft (52 metres) long. Walk on out of the village. At the end of the houses the surfaced road deteriorates to a stony track, and following this uphill slightly leads to a cross-tracks.

Turn right here for a few metres, and then go left along the margin of the field. This track leads to a sunken path between hedges, which soon begins to climb. This tunnel-like path reaches a stile and emerges at the foot of the steep scarp slope. Go over the stile and head diagonally left up the grassy slope, where cowslips grow in large numbers. Views rapidly open out over Alciston, Berwick and the Arlington Reservoir, and the North Downs may be visible in the distance.

At the top of this steep climb, go over the stile and head on diagonally left and slightly uphill to the top of the ridge. Here turn left to follow the path heading south-east. This is the South Downs Way, and we soon reach a small gate and a kissing gate with the acorn sign of the Way. Keep straight ahead along this track, passing a path off to the left signposted to Berwick. Down to our right is a huge dry valley, but further over to the right is the sea. As our path begins to descend, we can see the Cuckmere Valley. The first buildings to be visible down in the valley are the hamlet of Litlington with its tiny church, and then Alfriston with its much bigger church, the 'Cathedral of the Downs'. Both of these village names, as well as Alciston contain the Old English 'tun' or 'ton', being the homesteads and settlements created by Aelfsige, Aelfric and Lytel respectively.

When the path reaches a meeting of five paths, and the South Downs Way goes straight ahead, take the second left, a stony track descending between blackthorn and gorse bushes. The worn, stony track begins to bend left but we fork right here along a grassy path between a wire fence on the left and a hedge on the right, to descend very steeply. This can become muddy and slippery after rain, but leads down to the flat plain and a road. Pass between bungalows and houses, with a playing field and the school on the right. At the end of North Road turn right to return to the starting point near the Market Cross.

June: Rodmell and Castle Hill

*Begin at the small village of
Rodmell for this
steeplechasing walk in East
Sussex, visiting three flint
churches in the main walk.
The optional 4 miles take
you round a famous nature
reserve. Be sure to take
binoculars on this walk.
Rodmell was once a fishing
port, but the land has silted
up to form the marshes on
which Virginia Woolf sadly
wandered and was lost. In
addition to Monk's House,
the home of Virginia Woolf,
many other buildings of
interest can be seen in the
village, and a gentle
perambulation round the
village is well worthwhile.*

Marbled White butterfly

Distance: 13 miles, with a shorter route of 9 miles if preferred.

Time: 6 hours (or 4 – 5 hours)

Terrain: Mostly gentle walking on clear paths up on the South Downs, but fairly steep climbs from Rodmell and from Telscombe. There are a few stiles but much of the route is on bridleways with small gates to enable horses to pass through.

Maps: Landranger 198 or Explorer 122.

Starting Point: Just beyond Rodmell Church, GR 421064. Rodmell can be reached via Kingston along the narrow road which leads from the A27 near Lewes along the west side of the River Ouse.

Access: Buses run to Rodmell from Lewes, which can be reached by train.

Refreshments: Available at the pub at Rodmell or in Lewes.

Nearest Town: Lewes, where there is an Information Centre (01273 483448).

Weather

As the Azores high pressure system will have reached its most northerly location, June is likely to be a warm month, especially as any influences from the continent will be warm or even hot. Settled spells of hot weather could be associated with the high pressure remaining fairly motionless for several days – as a blocking high. This type of weather would give early morning mist and dew, but after a few days may provide enough heat to generate thunderstorms. These are especially likely if southerly winds from France bring extra heat into southern England.

June 24 is called Midsummer Day, though June 21st is the longest day of the year and also the summer solstice when the sun reaches its most northerly point. The long hours of daylight help to make June the sunniest month of the year, with an average of about 230 hours of sunshine in Sussex. Hours of daylight will be about 17 hours each day, and the normal, daily maximum temperature will be about 25C.

If high pressure persists, dry spells and drought may be experienced, as has happened several times in the 1990s. In 54BC, when Julius Caesar was on his second campaign in southern England, he commented on the smallness of the harvests because of the dry winds. This would have been the effect of a blocking high.

The Countryside

'A swarm of bees in May is worth a load of hay,
A swarm of bees in June is worth a silver spoon,
A swarm of bees in July is not worth a fly.'

A swarm of bees is generally thought to be caused or affected by good, sunny weather, and therefore for the farming communities a swarm might indicate the dry weather suitable for making hay and ripening crops.

Another old country saying relevant to June is, 'St Barnabas Day on 11th of June, mow your first grass.' Most farmers would hope to have cut the first load of hay much earlier than this.

At this time of year many plants have grown to their maximum height and crops are ripening. Some fields in this part of Sussex are used for grazing animals and others for arable. Crops until a few years ago would have been almost entirely cereals, but in recent years rape has become important because of the guaranteed price offered by the Common Agricultural Policy of the EU, and so fields of yellow flowers add to the colours of the countryside. Also, and for the same reason of profit, there are now a few fields of flax which are beginning to show their blue flowers. On the footpaths, nettles and brambles are stretching up and across, to waylay walkers, especially if wearing shorts. Wild flowers are still colourful along the lanes and hedgerows, and butterflies will become more numerous, especially in sunny spells. Other insects have also increased, which helps the rapid growth of many thousands of young birds which are being fed by their hard-working parents, who spend 16 or 17 hours per day catching insects. Birdsong is still quite common, though perhaps less persistent than last month.

Monks House

Virginia and Leonard Woolf lived in this house from 1919 until Virginia died in 1941, though Leonard remained here until his death in 1969. It is open from 2pm to 5.30pm on Wednesdays and Saturdays from April to the end of October. The house dates from 1707 or earlier, and was still quite primitive in 1919. They modernised it and added extra rooms. Much of the interior was designed and furnished with the help of Virginia's sister, Vanessa Bell, and Duncan Grant, both of whom were well known and successful artists. The gardens were enjoyed by both Virginia and Leonard, but he worked hard at it with the help of a full-time gardener. The lodge in the garden was Virginia's writing room. Adjacent to the garden is the village school and church of St Peter. Much of the church is Norman, dating from the 12th century, and the 13th-century tower is topped by a pyramid spire.

Southease Church

There has been a church here since at least AD966, when King Edgar issued a charter granting the church and the manor to Hyde Abbey at Winchester. It is especially noted for its round tower, one of only three in Sussex, the other two being at Piddinghoe and in Lewes. The original church was much larger, with the chancel extending on to what is now the small village green. Only the nave of this original church remains. On the north wall are faded 13th-century paintings depicting scenes from a Life of Christ, with clearer paintings on the west wall.

Castle Hill National Nature Reserve

Much of the land in the reserve has not been ploughed, enabling a wide variety of flowers to survive here, and in their turn, these have attracted insects and birds. Up to 30 different species of plants can sometimes be found in one square metre, and amongst the common flowers are salad burnet, vetches, centaury, small scabious and scarlet pimpernel. A wealth of chalk-loving grasses and flowers will be seen around here. The reserve is also noted for its bird life, including partridge, linnet, skylark, corn bunting, meadow pipit, whitethroat, stonechat, kestrel and yellowhammer. This reserve is managed by English Nature and covers about 45 hectares of hills and valleys. A permit is required to wander through the reserve, but we follow the public bridleway which leads straight across the reserve.

Sussex Downs

This Area of Outstanding Natural Beauty was designated in 1966 and covers an area of 983sq km. The AONB extends from Eastbourne to Chichester, and inland to Petworth.

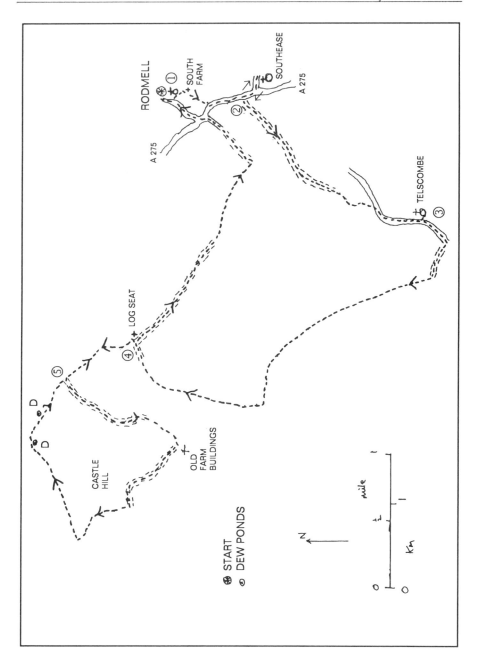

The Walk

Walk along the village street from the car park (1), passing the National Trust property Monks House, which was the home of Virginia and Leonard Woolf. Turn left to the church and go through the churchyard to a stile in the far right corner. Pass alongside the barn of South Farm and follow the track leading up to the road. Turn left and walk along the road for about 400 metres. Our onward route crosses the road (2) and follows the track leading south-westwards and up a dry valley, but before this, continue along the road for another 200 metres and turn left to visit the small flint church at Southease.

After this detour, retrace your steps and proceed up the dry valley, along the track leading steadily uphill, passing the barns in Cricketing Bottom. At the top of the hill reach a narrow road and turn right along this to the village of Telscombe and the church of St Lawrence – the third and last church on the route (3). Parts of this flint church date from the late 12th century. There are several flint houses in the village, which is dominated by the Stud Farm, where bed and breakfast accommodation is available.

From the church, pass the youth hostel and climb steeply out of the village. Where the road ends, turn right along the track leading to a couple of houses. Just before reaching these houses, turn right off the drive and pass through a small gate. One of the many chalkland dry valleys slopes down to our right, with the sheltered village of Telscombe at the bottom.

Our path leads straight ahead on a fairly level route, through another gate and along a grassy track, with wide open views away to the right. Continue straight ahead for more than a mile in a north-westerly direction, with views of Rottingdean back to the left, and Brighton in the distance. A large barn may be seen silhouetted on the skyline and we will walk past it in an hour or so.

The path passes between two old buildings and then bends round to the right, to climb steadily up to the barn. There are great views all round, with the sea and coast beyond Newhaven coming into sight. Just beyond the barn, a concrete track begins alongside the relics of a wartime building.

Short Cut

The concrete track soon turns right and this is the shorter route back to Rodmell, although if you are looking for a brief rest, about 30 metres ahead (4) is a huge log converted into a seat. It has a plaque to say that it is was designed by pupils from Northease Manor School in memory of David Cribbs (1944-1991) of Iford. From here are superb views east to Lewes, Mount Caburn near Glyndebourne and along the Downs towards Eastbourne.

Our route ahead is now the South Downs Way. It heads southeastwards and descends along the concrete track. A deep dry valley down to the right is called Whiteway Bottom, beyond it is the skyline along which we walked an hour ago. After a mile, at a T-junction, the main concrete track turns left, and we go straight ahead through a gate and along a field margin. At the bottom of the field cross a track into the next field. We go downhill at first, and then have to climb up to the corner and a gate, beyond which is a hedged path.

At the narrow road turn left and go downhill between the banks

The South Downs Way with terracettes on a scarp slope

with plants and hedges, and probably the noise of twittering birds. At the main road, go straight across, passing the Abergavenny Arms on the left. Walk down the village street, passing the interesting variety of houses – flint, hung tiles, some clapboard and a little thatch – to return to the car park and the starting point.

Longer Route

For the longer walk around Castle Hill, go past the seat, through the gate and turn left along the South Downs Way. Follow the broad path of the South Downs Way along the top of the scarp, with the steep, grassy slope down to the right. After half a mile, reach a major cross-paths, with a path going down the scarp to Kingston near Lewes, and the South Downs Way going straight ahead.

Turn left here (5), through a gate by a cattle grid, and follow the track as it meanders down the valley into Balsdean Bottom. At a gate and a barn continue ahead along the valley floor, through the field to a small gate. Cross the next field to a gate and then take a slight right bend as the path leads on towards the large shed and skeletal buildings.

Just before these buildings is another gate, and 30 metres beyond this, turn right along a grassy track to yet another gate. Beyond this is a clear path along the right side of a dry valley (Falmer Bottom). To the right is a fence bordering the Castle Hill National Nature Reserve. The slope and path margins are covered with grasses and wild flowers, including ox-eye daisies, scabious, the tall yellow agrimony and purple flowers of knapweed. Butterflies include the marbled white and small blue. There are places with rabbit holes and these are often surrounded by bare earth and exposed chalk – here and elsewhere on Castle Hill.

We reach a gate on the right, and go through here into the National Nature Reserve. Walk up a dry valley with characteristic chalkland grassy slopes on each side. The path becomes steeper as we walk on up this dry valley to an area with abundant wild flowers, gorse and prolific blackberry bushes in late summer. At the notice board which indicates the end of the nature reserve, we leave through the gate. Turn right here. After about 300 metres we join the South Downs Way coming in from the left, and keep straight ahead through a gate. Continue along the grassy track of the Way, with yet another large dry valley down to our left. At a stile and a gate, Juggs

Road goes straight on and down to Kingston near Lewes, but we turn right past a dew pond. There is now a different dry valley (Balsdean Bottom again) on our right. Pass another dew pond in a clump of bushes on the left, and go straight on through the next gate to a major cross-paths. The steep descent to Kingston goes left, the South Downs Way goes straight ahead and the track down to Balsdean Bottom goes right.

This is where we began the circuit of Castle Hill, but now we keep straight along the Way, retracing our steps to reach the log seat mentioned and seen earlier. Turn right to this seat, and then left along the concrete track to follow the South Downs Way down towards Rodmell. Follow the directions already given in the short cut.

Rodmell Church seen from the garden of Monks House

July: Kingley Vale

This walk is through woods, downland, and the National Nature Reserve at Kingley Vale, with its famous yew woods and Bronze Age burial mounds.

Housemartin

Distance: 8½ miles, or 7½ if taking the short cut.

Time: About 4 hours, more if spending time in the reserve.

Terrain: One steep climb and other more gentle ascents and descents. The paths can be muddy in places.

Maps: Landranger 197 or Explorer 120.

Starting Point: Car park on the right just past St Andrew's Church, West Stoke, GR 825087. The village is best reached from the A286 Midhurst to Chichester Road. If driving southwards, turn right in Mid Lavant, and take a minor road signposted to Funtington. Follow this road for 1½ miles to West Stoke. The small flint church is at the far end of the village.

Access: Buses run from Chichester to Stoughton (Monday to Saturday).

Refreshments: Available at the pub in Stoughton.

Nearest Town: Chichester, and it has a Tourist Information Centre (tel. 01243 77588).

Weather

South-eastern England will be the hottest part of the country this month, with average temperatures of about 17°C and daily maxima often reaching up to 25°C. Pressure is generally higher over the south of England than further north, though the anticyclones occasionally build up and affect the entire country. If the high pressure persists then droughts will occur, but several parts of Sussex are fortunate in having good groundwater supplies from the chalky areas. If southerly winds develop, excessive heat can be brought from as far south as the Sahara, and this brings reddish dust which will be brought down as red rain if there is a shower.

Anticyclonic weather can also be associated with the development of land and sea breezes. As the land heats during the day it becomes warmer than the sea and winds begin to blow inland. These will feel cool, and can affect not only sunbathers on the beach but also all areas a few miles inland. At night the process is reversed as the land cools faster than the sea, causing winds to blow out from land to the sea. As a contrast to the hot weather, rainy weather can occur and occasional thunderstorms develop during this month. Depressions can sometimes bring rain, too, but even though the 15th July is St Swithin's Day, there is unlikely to be a prolonged spell of rain. Certainly there is very little truth or reliability in the old saying, 'St Swithin's Day if you bring rain, for forty days it will remain.'

The Countryside

Greenery may remain in the woods, hedges and some well-watered meadows, but much of the countryside will be turning golden as the cereal crops begin to ripen. Fields of rape will have mostly lost their yellow colour as the oil pods replace the flowers, but the other oil crop, flax (linum anglicum), will still be showing its delicate blue flowers. Wild flowers are still in evidence along hedges, lanes and field margins, and the reduced use of herbicide has enabled the red poppies to reappear in many of the fields. St John's wort is in flower – in former years this plant was used to treat wounds. It was also used to ward off evil spirits, if it could be hung over a picture of St John on the 23rd June (St John's Day). Gardens are very colourful at this time of year, and amongst the most notable plants are the hydrangeas, all pink in this chalky area where alkali soils are widespread.

Birdsong can still be heard, though less frequently than in June and May, and amongst the downland songbirds, linnets, skylarks and yellowhammers are most characteristic. Warblers too are singing, even though the small birds are not easily seen in the dense vegetation at this time of year. Some species, such as finches, starlings, rooks, jackdaws and tits, are in flocks as family groups merge. Food supplies are abundant and so competition for food is less than at other times of the year. Swallows and martins are twittering overhead in many locations.

Butterflies are quite numerous, including the meadow brown, marbled white, red admiral and the whites, although generally there are fewer butterflies than in the past. For some species this is the time of the second breeding period, and the butterflies are likely to be the grandchildren of those seen in late spring.

Kingley Vale National Nature Reserve

Kingley Vale National Nature Reserve contains one of the finest yew forests in Europe (with 30 000 specimens). The reserve covers an area of 150 hectares of South Down chalkland and adjacent valleys. Part is owned by English Nature, but the eastern part is leased from the Edward James Foundation. The reserve is managed by English Nature, the body which advises the government on conservation, promotes the conservation of wild life and natural features, and identifies Sites of Special Scientific Interest, as well as managing National Nature Reserves.

Yew Trees

The most massive yew trees, according to legend, were planted to commemorate victory over the Vikings in AD859. Whatever the legend may be, it is certainly true that some of the yews are 500 years old, though the majority are from 50 to 250 years old. About 20 of the very old yews remain. The wood is very hard and has been used for making furniture, drinking vessels and posts, and also for longbows. These bows needed very strong men to pull them, and they were often used by lying down on one's back and using the legs to push the bow whilst pulling the string with both hands. Yew trees are either male or female. Females have red berries in autumn, and males have tiny cones which produce pollen in winter. Many of the yews are growing on the coombe rock, which is the loose rock and soil washed down the chalk slopes by solifluction resulting from freeze/thaw activity during the Ice Age. At this period the climate was much colder, similar to Arctic Canada today, and repeated freezing and thawing of the rock caused it to disintegrate and the fragments to slide downhill, when lubricated by melt water.

St Mary's Church, Stoughton

The oldest part of this cruciform Saxon church is the chancel, some of which dates from about 1050. There are no aisles, and the south transept was made into a tower in the 14th century. The church is much older than other buildings in the village, where only one house is earlier than the 16th century. The graveyard may formerly have been the location of a larger building, though the church is still quite impressive for such a small village. Possibly the village was much bigger in the past, earlier houses having been removed after the time of the Black Death.

St Mary's Church

The Walk

From the car park (1), take the stony track leading northwards between two fields, and the smell of flowers and crops and the noise of
birdsong will soon enable us to forget the traffic and the roads. My
first birdsong on this walk was a whitethroat singing lustily from the
top of a bush alongside the path. Pheasants, blackcaps and other
birds were noisy, including skylark and yellowhammer, and the
wild flowers alongside the path were colourful and varied (white
campion, thistles, poppies, ladies bedstraw, St John's wort). Crops
will be ripening in the fields alongside.

This wide track is ideal for use in July as even the lush summer
growth cannot spread across the width of the path, and so nettles
etc. are not a problem. At the first patch of woodland the path may
become muddy, especially after heavy rain, but we soon pass out
into the open again, with woods on the left and a farm field to the
right.

At the cross-paths and gate (2) is the entry to Kingley Vale National Nature Reserve, and just beyond the stile is a sculpture by
Walter Bailey, carved from one yew tree in 1955 and representing

The entrance to Kingley Vale

The Spirit of Kingley Vale. Close by is the Information Centre and Field Museum, which is generally open, and contains masses of interesting information about the reserve, especially remarkable being the total of over 200 flowering plants, including 12 species of orchids. There are 57 species of breeding birds as well as 39 species of breeding butterflies (out of the English total of 58). In a wet summer there are fewer butterflies, but there is more birdsong to compensate for this fact. In the museum is a hands-on display to show footprints, and if there are patches of mud in the woods, look into them to see if you can spot any deer prints. There is also a display showing the most dangerous animal to visit Kingley Vale (look in the mirror).

Our walk follows the line of the Nature Trail, for which a very interesting, coloured booklet is generally available. The well-worn track leads into woodland, and there will doubtless be grey squirrels rushing about in front of us. Pass the soil pit, which is number one in the Nature Trail. Here there is an information board explaining that on top of the chalk rock is a layer of coombe rock. The woodland is rich and diverse as we follow the arrows straight ahead.

At post 4 take the right turn beneath the yew trees and walk on past the yew grove information board to post 5. Continue into more open woodland, where the wild roses are likely to be in glorious flower. The hilltop straight ahead comes into view just before we detour right at post number 6 to pass under a fine, old oak tree. This is a very different habitat from that associated with the dark and gloom of the yew grove, where few birds live. The oak is a wonderful habitat for a large number of birds and insects, and is well described on the information board as a supermarket for wild life, able to support up to 200 varieties of insect life and up to 20 species of bird.

Walk through an open glade and keep straight on past the pointer to numbers 7, 8 and 9, which are to the right. Reach a stile and gate at the foot of the steep slope. A useful information board points out what can be seen on the slope ahead. This excellent provision of information is similar to what is often found in National Parks in the USA, and on some National Trust land, too. It is certainly an idea which could be used in far more locations in Britain.

Various ecosystems can be seen on the slope ahead, with chalk grassland, a patch of yews of about 80 years old, more yews of about 100 and the lighter green of ash and whitebeam in amongst the dark yews. The ash tree will grow quickly to fill in gaps when yews die.

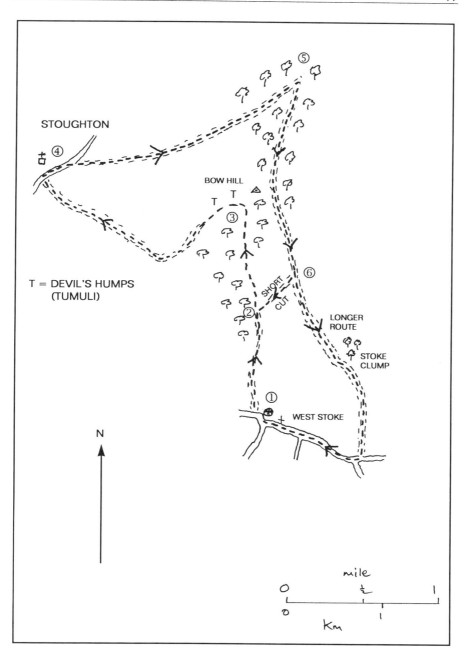

STOUGHTON

BOW HILL

T = DEVIL'S HUMPS
(TUMULI)

SHORT CUT

LONGER
ROUTE

STOKE
CLUMP

WEST STOKE

N

mile

Old Celtic field boundaries (called lynchets) are on the lower slopes, and the mixed woodland up on the top of the chalk hill can be seen. That is where we are heading next.

If you do not fancy the steep slope, follow the numbered posts as they circle round to the right and then swing left to climb up to the top of the slope ahead and reach the grassy area near the Devil's Humps.

If you are going straight ahead, leave the Nature Trail, go over the stile and up the grassy slope, on which numerous small flowers will be seen. Yellowhammers are likely to be noisy in this area, and green woodpeckers will be laughing away. Birdsong in this beautiful setting may include robins, blackbirds, and warblers. A kestrel may be quartering the hillside looking for his next meal. Continue up the grassy slope and go over a stile into the woods, where it is even steeper and often slippery after rain – quite a testing slope. The last time I was here, whilst resting beneath a yew to recover my breath, a young green woodpecker flew into the next tree to give me my closest ever view of this handsome, noisy bird. Young birds of all species do not seem to have the same fear or shyness as the adults.

At the top of this slope (3), we emerge out on to a grassy patch where the Tansley Stone is located. This is a memorial to Sir Arthur George Tansley FRS the first chairman of the Nature Conservancy Council (now replaced by English Nature), who created this nature reserve. Fine views look out down into the grassy coombe and above the woodlands we have walked through, as well as out to the coastal inlets and the Isle of Wight over to the right.

The grassy area will have a variety of wildflowers, and these may include a few which are different from elsewhere on this walk, including some heather. Tormentil (hoary cinquefoil) and bird's foot trefoil are common here, as are the ubiquitous brambles. Here is a 1.2 hectares-patch of chalky heathland, an unusual and quite rare habitat. The chalk is covered with a thin layer of clay, a residual soil remaining from thousands of years of erosion of the chalk.

Views from the open patch of grassland include Portsdown with its radio masts, and Pagham Harbour. Also near the right-hand end of this grassy area are two tumuli, bowl barrows which are two of the Devil's Humps, Bronze Age burial tombs dating from about 1500BC. The other Devil's Humps are at the opposite, left-hand end of the grassy patch and are known as bell barrows because of their shape. Marker post 18 is near these tumps.

There are excellent views from on top of these mounds and the grassy area around here could provide a good location for a picnic, though it might be too early in the walk. On a hot day there is likely to be a refreshing breeze blowing here, but one advantage of walking in the summer is that it is warm enough to sit down and have a leisurely picnic, as long as there are not too many flies or wasps to ruin it.

For the onward walk we pass to the left of the bell barrows on a very clear, level track leading into the woods. Ignore the numbered Nature Trail, signposted downhill at this point. Our track is a public bridleway, with some stony and some muddy patches. When we reach a cross-paths, keep straight ahead, as far as the T-junction by an open field.

Now out of the woods, turn right along the track to follow the margin of the field, and we are soon joined by a track coming in from the right (also coming from the top of the hill near the tumps). We soon reach a stony track, signposted public bridleway, and descend through the woods, quite steeply in parts, before emerging into open ground, and having splendid views over Stoughton, down in the valley. Just continue downhill along this stony track, which gradually levels off. Pass a memorial to a Polish fighter pilot who crashed in this field during the Second World War then continue to the road. We reach the road between Jeremys and Tythe Barn House, two of the lovely buildings in this village. Turn right along the road.

Walk along the village street in Stoughton, a small, flinty village, hidden away in a fold of the Downs. Off to the left is a renovated flint barn on the track to St Mary's Saxon church (4). The local garden walls and the church are of flint.

Continue through the village, past the Hare and Hounds, also a flint building. Near the end of the village look for the path on the right. Turn right at Old Bartons, passing the main building on the left with the barns on the right. Bear left along a stony track leading out into open country, with woods on the hills ahead. The track is level at first, but after passing the barns on the right, the steady climb begins. Along this stretch of the walk yellowhammers and pied wagtails are likely to be seen, and there will be swallows and martins flying near the barns or out over the fields. Pheasants are quite common around here, especially near the margins of the woods. Harebells, white campion, ragwort and toadflax are amongst the wild flowers growing alongside the footpath.

Ignore the footpath going off to the left. Our stony track becomes grassy and narrows as it passes between two wire fences on the final ascent before reaching the woods on the left of the path. The blind end of the dry valley is down to our right. At the cross-paths just inside the wood, where five ways meet, we go ahead and slightly left, following a public bridleway sign. Walk along the broad, stony and grassy track, between beech trees on both sides. Take a slight right bend and then a slight left bend, ignoring the grassy track going diagonally left and the grassy tracks at right angles on the right. Reach a gate and then a major meeting of tracks, where we turn right (5), more than a right angle, to head in a southerly direction along a broad track. Good views open up to the left, especially where the very steep slope is close to the path. The track divides but we fork right, not left alongside the fence and the edge of the woods.

Along this track we soon reach a major cross-paths, where there is a notice board welcoming us to the Kingley Vale Nature Reserve. Our onward route is turning left here, beginning to go downhill, and open fields will soon appear on our left. If you wish to visit the triangulation point on the top of this hill (Bow Hill, 676ft), keep straight ahead for about 200 metres and it is in a small clearing a few metres to the right of the path. Then retrace your steps to the cross-paths by the notice board.

The track is sunken for a distance, between yew and hawthorn trees, and as the views open out, Chichester Cathedral will be prominent. Away to the left will be seen the B2141, and beyond it the masts on the top of Trundle Hill, near Goodwood. Orchids grow in a small grassy area to the left of the path. Shortly beyond this we emerge from the bottom of the woodland and follow the track between farm fields. Poppies brighten up the wheat field, and skylarks are noisy overhead. There were only partridges in the field to the left of the path, where stone curlews nested until about 30 years ago.

Short Cut

Reach a crossing point of bridleways (6) and turn right for the shorter return to the starting point. Go along this path as far as the main gate into Kingley Vale and there turn left to walk back to the small car park.

Longer Route

For the slightly longer walk, keep straight ahead at the cross-paths. Follow the narrow bridleway between cropped fields and begin to climb slightly. Blackthorn on the left of the path can be showing its first green berries, and this narrow path can be quite muddy where it is almost covered by trees arching overhead. The path comes out into open land and is much drier, and views open out again. At the top of the climb the Isle of Wight becomes visible over to the right, possibly with boats to be seen sailing up Spithead.

The path is along the right side of a small wood, Stoke Clump. In this wood are several uprooted trees showing chalk on their roots, but many young trees are growing up to replace them. Walk on down to a broader track, and then reach the road where we turn right.

Walk past the buildings of West Stoke village. Just beyond Lye Lane is the flint-walled village hall, where cream teas are served on Sundays from June to September. Be alert for traffic along this road. Soon you reach West Stoke House, with the vineyard on the right. Next to it is the tiny flint church of St Andrew. It has a short tower with a pyramid tile cap. The nave walls date from the 11th century. Its most interesting contents are the memorial to Adrian Stoughton and family, from 1635, and a memorial mural to Sir John Leslie Turing. There may be a swallow's nest in the porch.

Continue along the road. After a few metres the road splits, with the left fork signposted to Ashley and Chichester. We, however, turn right along the narrow road to reach the car park.

August: Rye

This invigorating walk
is across the flat,
low-lying Rye
marshes, passing the
ruins of Camber
Castle, and a church
with a memorial to
local lifeboatmen. The
land has been created
from the sea and
remains very
windswept. Even in
August warm clothing
may be required.
Much of the area
crossed is a nature
reserve and binoculars are essential on this walk.

Little Tern

Distance: 10½ miles, or 8 miles for the short cut.

Time: 5 hours (3 – 4 hours)

Terrain: Very flat, but there may be muddy patches as well as stretches
of shingle to walk over, and a few stiles to be climbed.

Maps: Landranger 189 or Explorer 125.

Starting Point: Rye, GR 917204, although an alternative starting point
could be at Rye Harbour, GR 943188, where there is free parking.

Access: Rye can be reached along the A259 from Hastings or from
Folkestone, and is also accessible by several bus services and by train.

Refreshments: Available in Rye, Rye Harbour or Winchelsea.

Nearest Tourist Information Centre: Rye (01797 226696)

Weather

Often the warmest month of the year, and the most popular month for holidays, August is not noted for the reliability of its weather. A good, settled spell is likely sometime during the month, and in 1995 a blocking high pressure system kept the weather very hot and dry until the bank holiday weekend when a long dry spell ended. Bank holiday weather is generally remembered, and one of the worst ever was in 1956, when cold weather and thunderstorms were recorded in many places. Royal Tunbridge Wells suffered from heavy hailstorms, which gave accumulations up to 2ft (60cms) in depth. That was exceptional, and average totals of precipitation for August in south-eastern England are about 60 to 70mm, compared with 70-80mm in south-west England and as much as 100mm in the hills of the north and the west. The Snowdon average is over 370mm.

'St Bartholomew brings the cold dew.' This old saying suggests that on the 24th August it is expected that an anticyclonic spell will bring mist and dew. This is certainly a possibility, but is more likely to occur in September.

Another saying for St Bartholomew's day is:
'If the 24th be fair and clear,
Then hope for a prosperous autumn that year.'

This could turn out to be true, but it would be a chance occurrence rather than a situation with any scientific explanation.

The Countryside

August is often the main harvest month and so dry spells of weather are particularly important for farmers, though less vital nowadays with modern machinery. This is the traditional month for school holidays. The practice arose because of the need in former times for entire families to work on the harvesting of crops, but nowadays, holidays are more likely to be spent at the seaside. Fortunately, the sea is at its hottest this month, averaging about 17°C. along the Sussex coast.

The Sussex countryside will be golden with ripe crops, or brown where already harvested and ploughed. Most trees are still green, though some horse chestnuts are beginning to show yellow on their leaves.

A few swallows, house martins, and warblers will still be seen, trying to feed themselves up for their long migratory flights. Many of the residents gather together in family groups which can then build up into flocks, especially in the case of starlings, finches, house sparrows and the tits. Gulls will still be evident around Rye, but the terns will have gone by the end of the month. August is a month of change, with summer residents finishing their breeding and leaving before the end of the month. Winter visitors have not yet arrived, but autumnal passage migrants may be seen here, such as turtle doves, yellow wagtails, wheatears or hobbies.

Many flowers are still in colour, even though they may be past their best, and the first blackberries will be ripening.

Rye

Rye is a picturesque hilltop town with narrow and cobbled streets climbing up from the River Rother. The many well-preserved old buildings include houses from medieval, Tudor and Georgian times. Mermaid Street is lined with houses from the 15th, 16th and 17th centuries, including the Mermaid Inn, which has a vaulted cellar from the 13th century. This inn was a famed haunt of smugglers in the 18th century, at which time there were as many as 40 000 involved in smuggling. Another old inn is The George, dating from 1575. One of Rye's most notable houses is the early 18th-century Lamb House, which was home to two authors, E.F. Benson and Henry James. It was Henry James who described Rye as 'a small and compact port'.

Rye was situated on the coast until the 16th century. Then the sea receded and the rivers silted up the harbour area, and the importance of the town declined. Some small craft can still reach Rye along the River Rother, the main stream, which is joined at Rye by the Brede and Tillingham.

The Ypres Tower was built about 1250, at the command of Henry III, to help defend the town, but after repeated attacks the French sacked Rye in 1377, though the tower survived. It was used as a prison from 1518 until the 19th century and was restored in 1928 to become a museum. Another ancient building to have survived is the church of St Mary the Virgin. Built of stone and flint, parts of the nave, aisles and arcades date from 1150, but the tower and chancel are from the 15th century. The tower contains one of the oldest

Ypres Tower

working clocks in England, having been in the church since 1562. The pendulum swings inside the church and the painted clock face has two figures which ring the bell on quarter hours, hence the name of Quarter Boys. The west window was presented by E.F. Benson, and there is a Burne-Jones window in the north aisle.

The Cinque Ports (Hastings, Romney, Hythe, Dover and Sandwich) originated in the 11th century, though Rye and Winchelsea were later added to this association. These were the key towns which helped the sovereign to defend this coastline against attack, and because of this they were exempt from taxes and could hold their own courts of law.

Church of the Holy Spirit, Rye Harbour

This stone church, with its distinctive, apsidal eastern end, dates from 1849 and contains memorials to the local lifeboatmen. Most moving is the tablet on the north wall, a memorial to the crew of the *Mary Stanford*. All 17 died whilst trying to help the *Alice* in November 1928. There is also a large memorial outside the church.

Martello Tower

The tower at Rye Harbour was one of 74 built along the coast between 1805 and 1810 to protect the country from attack by Napoleon. This particular tower was built in 1807. The brick walls are almost 6ft thick, and on top was a platform for a cannon. The towers were named after a fort at Cape Mortella in Corsica, which was used against the attacking Britons in 1794.

Rye Harbour Nature Reserve

The reserve contains shingle deposits, meadowland, salt marsh and former gravel pits, and is noted for its vegetation, animals and especially bird life. Amongst the noted animals are the marsh frog which can be heard croaking during the summer months, and the brown hare which may be seen on the beach. The greatest wealth of the reserve is generally considered to be its rich bird life, which includes breeding colonies of terns and other ground nesting birds, together with an assortment of migrating birds which pass through this area in spring and autumn. Large numbers of ducks, geese and waders spend the winter here, as well as a few raptors, merlin, short-eared owl, hobby and hen harrier.

The shingle ridges have been built up by a series of massive storms and recorded history makes it possible to date the formation of these ridges during recent centuries. The colonisation of these ridges by differing forms of vegetation has been carefully studied and the speed and order of the vegetation succession is now well known.

Winchelsea

Winchelsea Beach was the old town on the coast, but many of the original houses are now buried beneath shingle, having been damaged by storms in1252 and finally overwhelmed by a great storm in 1288. The king had already acquired land in Iham to build a new town in a safer location.

The modern town of Winchelsea is inland, on top of what used to be the coastal cliff, and is spacious and symmetrical, built to a gridiron plan – an early example of a planned town. It was laid out by Edward I, who was Lord Warden of the Cinque Ports in 1283. A few old buildings survive but the majority are from the last 100 years. Part of the Court Hall dates back to the 14th century, but it was drastically

Winchelsea

restored in the 16th century and later – but now contains the museum. Below it are the old dungeons.

St Thomas's Church is the 14th-century chancel of an original church and contains some outstanding 20th-century stained glass windows. Older relics are numerous, and it is worth obtaining the guide book if a lengthy visit is intended. Note particularly the tombs in the north wall, containing three effigies older than the church, which probably came here from the church at Old Winchelsea. With the churchyard, the church occupies one complete block of the original planned town, but only the chancel and side chapels have remained, and the transepts and nave have disappeared, if they were ever completed. The original town walls have gone, but three of the four gates have survived. Many of the attractive houses in the town have hung tiles, or clapboard walls.

Camber Castle

This 16th-century castle, now managed by English Heritage, was built by Henry VIII to defend Rye Harbour as he feared a Papal invasion after his split with the Roman Catholic Church. It was built on

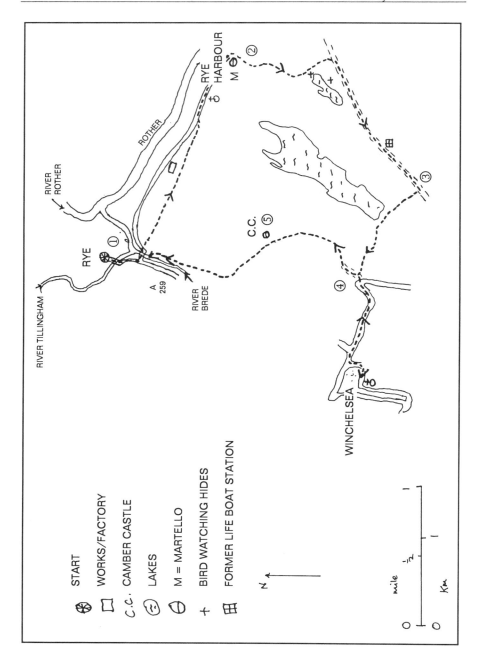

an existing gun tower located on a shingle spit and was completed in 1543, but was abandoned in 1642 because of the receding coastline. It gradually became a ruin, but this has helped to make it unique as it was never modified. In 1967 it was taken over by the state, and was closed for safety reasons. Repairs have been carried out and the castle is now open on Saturday afternoons in July, August and September. Several flowers grow on the walls of the castle which are particularly adapted to grow in these conditions, including wall pennywort and the yellow-flowered wallflower.

The Walk

Start from Rye (1) and leave town along the A259 towards Winchelsea, with the River Tillingham on the left and the white smock windmill on the right. Turn left along the road towards Rye Harbour. Cross over the River Brede just above its confluence with the Tillingham, and notice the lock which is used to prevent sea water from flowing up this river at high tides.

Where the road bends left there is a riverside path on the right – the route of our return walk – and just beyond a small car parking space is a stile and a public footpath sign. This is our route to Rye Harbour. Go over the stile and along the path between two hedges along the embankment of the former railway line. This line opened in March 1854 to link the tar, shingle and concrete works at Rye Harbour with the main railway line, and remained in use until February 1960. Reach a stile by an iron gate and go straight ahead, on to an open, grassy area grazed by sheep and their lambs. Camber Castle will be visible over to the right, and we will visit that later.

After another stile the path splits, with a right turn towards Camber, but we keep straight ahead towards Rye Harbour. There are now factories to the left and pools of water on both sides, and ragwort, teasels, viper's bugloss and probably many gulls around here. White arrows on the marker posts point us ahead and then slightly left, which leads us through to the road.

Turn right here to walk along the verge, visiting the Rye Harbour Church of the Holy Spirit, with its memorials to the lifeboatmen. Then walk on to the free car park and information centre near the Martello Tower (2).

Walk on the road into Frenchman's Beach Holiday Village, passing to the left of the Martello Tower. At the end of the Holiday Village, go over a footbridge across a channel and follow the path along the top of an embankment, out on to what used to be marshes, but are now open fields of crops, probably ready for harvest. Early signs of the varied bird life to be seen on this walk will already be apparent – yellow wagtails, whitethroats, sedge warblers, corn buntings, kestrels, are amongst the birds likely to be seen around here. Reach the edge of the nature reserve and turn left, still following the embankment. There is marshy ground to the left and a lake, Ternery Pool, to the right. The path is lined with wild flowers, many of which will have seed heads by the end of the month.

On the right we reach the Ray Parkes' (a doctor at Brede) Memorial Hide, which provides a view along the lake. Birds likely to be seen are black-headed gulls, cormorants, Canada geese, tufted ducks, mallards, coots, moorhens, little grebes (or dabchicks) and terns. Islands in this lake are used for nesting, though many birds nest along the lake margins and in areas away from the lake, many of them moving out from the relative safety of the nature reserve. Nesting birds here include the terns, black-headed gulls, and also redshanks, ringed plover and lapwings.

Scrunch along the shingly path, where you should find sea kale. This grows straight out of the shingle, as do most of the plants which survive in this fairly hostile environment. There's little or no soil, a lot of wind, salty air, and it's very dry as any water quickly runs through the stones.

We reach a narrow tarmac road used by the Environmental Agency lorries involved in coastal maintenance, and here we turn right. To the right and left are areas of shingle, with bird life as well as some interesting plants: more sea kale, the yellow-horned poppy, valerian, and viper's bugloss (Echium vulgare, a member of the borage family). An information board headed 'Adapt and Survive' gives facts about these plants, as well as drawings which will aid identification. On the right we reach a second hide, the Crittall Hide, named after Guy Crittall, which provides excellent views of the Ternery Pool.

Continuing along the tarmac, we walk on past the old lifeboat house. This was the location of the lifeboat station mentioned in the Church of Holy Spirit in Rye Harbour. As the shingle area becomes narrower, we reach a notice board to indicate the edge of the nature reserve. The wire fence on our right turns right (3), and so do we. Following a signpost and yellow arrow pointing to a footpath to the right, we walk across 50 metres of shingle to reach a grassy path on an embankment. Pass a wooden seat on the right and continue along the embankment, between grasses and wild flowers, with cropped fields on both sides.

Reach a cross-paths and keep straight ahead, with a large lake, Long Pit, now on our right, possibly with swallows and swifts flying over it (although swifts will have departed by mid-month). At the end of the lake, go over a stile and keep straight ahead across a small field and another stile. Follow the stony track to a cross-paths, where a stony drive goes left. We keep straight ahead, over a stile and across a small field to a stile and footbridge. Keep ahead across the field, often used for caravans, and through a gate into the next field. Walk along the left side of this field to reach a stile and footbridge, then follow the path round the edge of the gardens to a stile. Turn left to walk to a stile and out on to a narrow road. Here is the point of decision (4), whether to turn left to walk into Winchelsea or turn right for the shorter route back to Rye.

Short Cut

Turn right along the road and after 150 metres fork right, following the main drive and a yellow arrow, to pass two houses on the right and then the farm buildings. Just past the farm the track splits, take the left fork. After 30 metres, at a gate, the drive splits again and again we take the left fork. Walk along a stony track to emerge on an open, grassy area, where linnets may be heard twittering. Other finches and starlings are also active around here.

The path winds across the grassy area to a stile and a gate. Before continuing straight ahead, detour right to visit Camber Castle (5). Then continue ahead on the path alongside a fence to our left, and at the end of the field go through an iron gate and straight ahead along an embankment, with drainage channels to right and left. The embankment soon bends right, before reaching the river. We follow this path near the river until reaching a stony drive, which we then follow out on to the road. Turn left to walk back into Rye, or turn right if you started from Rye Harbour.

Longer Route

Turn left along the narrow road – it soon joins a bigger road. Turn right here and use the pavement to walk towards Winchelsea, which can be seen on the hilltop ahead. At the main road turn left, signposted to Hastings, and go left again at the first turning. Climb a few steps and then continue on the narrow road up into Winchelsea. Go through the archway, which is the Strand Gate, one of the three surviving gates, and along the east-west trending road. On the left is The Lookout, with fine views. The first house was once lived in by Ellen Terry.

At the first crossroads look right and left, along the roads which run north to south as part of the rectangular plan. At the second crossroads, turn right along Castle Street for a few metres. On the right is the old Town Well, from 1851, and just beyond this is The Armoury. Retrace your steps along this road and cross High Street to go along St Thomas's Street, with the church on the right, situated in the middle of the original grid plan. Pass an oak tree commemorating the coronation of Queen Elizabeth in 1953, and several hung tile buildings, so typical of the Wealden architecture. On the left is the stone-built Greyfriars Lodge and then a school, just before the end of the road. Here a gate marks the entrance to Greyfriars, the site of a former monastery. The main house was built in the 19th century though much modernised this century, and some ruins of the 14th-century chapel still remain.

Retrace your steps to the High Street and turn left, heading west, with the church now on the left. On the right is the old Court House, now a museum, open mornings and afternoons from Tuesday to Saturday, and afternoons on Sundays. There is an admission charge. At the crossroads the main road bends left, but we keep straight on to reach the A259, Rye to Hastings road. Turn left here and soon pass John Wesley's chapel (1785), where he preached in January 1789 and again in 1790, when he was 87. Across the road from this chapel are the remnants of a house believed to have belonged to the Black Friars, who came to Winchelsea in 1318. Adjacent to this ruin is the town cricket pitch. Beyond the chapel take the first left, Back Lane, and walk to the church. There is a useful information board in front of the church, close to the famous Wesley tree. He preached under an ash tree (not the present one) which stood on this site on 7th October 1790. Then visit the church of St Thomas the Martyr, which may look rather dull from the outside, but the inside will more than make up for that. Outside the church can be seen remnants, part destroyed and part unfinished, of the much bigger church which had been planned.

Retrace your steps to the Strand Gate and walk down to the main road. Turn right and then right again to take the road towards Winchelsea Beach, and back to (4 again) the route described earlier. Follow the short cut route to walk past Camber Castle, and back to Rye.

September: Clayton

*This downland walk is not
at all strenuous. It visits two
churches and passes two
windmills.*

Distance: 9 miles (short cut
route of 7 miles, omitting the
walk to Ditchling Beacon and
North Bottom).

Time: 4 hours (short cut 3
hours)

Terrain: One climb and one
descent of the escarpment
plus other small hills.

Lapwing

Maps: Landranger 198 and Explorer 122.

Starting Point: The car park at Jack and Jill windmills, Clayton, GR
304134. This is close to Pyecombe, where the A273 joins the A23, the
main London to Brighton road.

Access: A regular bus service runs from Brighton.

Refreshments: Pubs in Pyecombe and Clayton. There is often an ice
cream van at Ditchling Beacon.

Nearest Towns: Hassocks and Hurstpierpoint

Nearest Tourist Information Centre: Brighton (01273 292599)

Weather

This is the first month of autumn and in most years it is a very changeable month, with spells of warm, settled weather and one or more periods of wet and windy weather. There is clear evidence that summer is over, though up on the Downs there will be pleasant days, alternating with wild, windswept conditions. The old saying, 'Fair on 1st September, fair for the month,' is unlikely to be true – a spell of anticyclonic weather, required to give fair weather, is almost certain to give way to cyclonic conditions sometime during the month. Historically, 1907 and 1919 show the extremes. Temperatures in south-east England reached 25°C on the 25th in 1907, whilst in 1919 there was widespread snow on the 20th of September. If anticyclonic weather dominates for several consecutive days, this enables local weather features to develop, and in the Downs this will be shown by variations between hilltops and valleys. Cold air rolls down hillsides and into the valley bottoms in the evenings, and this cold air accumulates and becomes much colder than the air above. This contributes to the formation of mist in the valleys, which can be looked down upon from the Downs if you are still out walking as darkness falls.

The Countryside

The cuckoos have gone and the swallows will be assembling on telegraph wires before setting off on their long journey to Africa. The parents, identifiable by their long tail feathers, go first, leaving all the first year birds, with shorter tail feathers, to find their own way on this long journey. Their close relatives the house martins tend to travel slightly later, and they, too, may have separate groups of parents and offspring. House martins often nest quite late into September or even October, and it has been known for parent birds to set off on their migration leaving unfledged chicks in the nests. It seems as though a sudden command tells the internal computer controlling the martins' migration that they must set off immediately. Resident birds may also migrate, but only over shorter distances. This month is a fairly quiet time in the bird world, with little singing to be heard, though pheasants will be calling noisily. Plant life is also dying down at this time, with wild flowers fading, and many of the farmers' crops having been harvested. Hedges and woods are still looking green, however, with old man's beard beginning to show up in the hedgerows. Elderberries and other berries are prolific in some locations, and there is plenty of life in the countryside, with many of the verges still looking overgrown. Bindweed flowers are in many of the hedges, and the feathery remnants of rosebay willowherb may be drifting around whenever the wind blows. The downlands have large numbers of grazing sheep, as well as cattle, and in the vales where cereals (except for some of the maize) have been harvested, ploughing has already begun. Rooks and gulls are likely to be flocking behind the tractors, looking for easy food. Other birds may be gathering in flocks, as is the case with several types of finches, lapwings and starlings.

Jack and Jill

Jack and Jill are already at the top of the hill, as these two remarkable windmills stand prominently on top of the South Downs. Jack is black, privately owned and not open to the public, but Jill is white and open to the public from 2 to 5pm on Sundays and bank holidays from May to September.

Jill

Jack is a large, brick tower mill built in 1866. There had already been a mill on this site for 100 years. Jack had a revolving cap which carried the sails and was in use until 1906.

Jill is a timber post-mill built in Brighton in 1821, and transported to its present site by a team of oxen in 1852. It ceased milling in 1906. The whole building, painted white, is automatically turned by the fan tackle to keep the sweeps facing the wind. Jill can grind 1cwt (50kg) of flour in approximately ten minutes. In recent years the Jack and Jill Windmill Society have successfully restored her to working order, and she produces some stoneground wholemeal flour.

St John Baptist Church

The Clayton church is noted for its collection of wall paintings, which probably once covered all four walls of the nave. They were only discovered in 1895. This flint church has been refaced with plaster in places, and the roof is covered with thin slabs of rock. Most of the nave and chancel are Norman. The paintings are thought to date from the 11th century, and as with so many wall paintings in churches, they depict gospel stories. These would not have been regarded merely as a work of art, but could have been used a form of teaching aid in the days when few people could read. The church is entered through what was probably originally a

Lych gate, Clayton

Norman doorway, and just inside is a step down into the church. It has been suggested that all churches dedicated to St John the Baptist have this type of step, to signify going down into the Jordan for baptism.

The lych-gate has a plaque mentioning that the local community was recorded in the Domesday Book in 1086. The lych-gate was restored in September 1944 – and you may notice that it has a stone slab roof, similar to parts of the church. The path leading to the church is made of ripple-marked stones, quarried at Horsham but formed originally as a sand deposit on a seabed or in a river.

Ditchling Beacon

The land near here was given to the National Trust by Sir Stephen Demetriadi in memory of his son who was killed in the Battle of Britain. On the hill was one of a series of 13th-century beacons which were intended to convey messages from the Sussex coast to London -supposedly in twenty minutes! Piles of wood were burnt at first, but in 1388 Edward III suggested the idea of having metal containers on the top of poles. The beacons were lit at the time of the Spanish Armada.

The beacon reaches 813ft (248 metres) and has the traces of a rampart of an Iron Age fort. This is about 2000 years old, and may have been used as a defensive fort against the invading Romans. The land all around is part of a SSSI, with areas of undisturbed grass where wild flowers thrive.

Pyecombe Church

This small, flint church dates from the 12th century. The nave and chancel are Norman and the lead font (one of only three in Sussex) is 12th century, and is large and deep, suitable for total immersion. The tower and the wooden pyramid cap (known as a Sussex cap) date from the early 13th century. The tapsel gate into the churchyard turns on a central pivot, and has recently been renovated. The house opposite this gate used to be the village smithy, where shepherds' crooks were made.

The Walk

Leave the far end of the car park (1) through a small gate, with Jack and Jill behind you. Follow the footpath sign to walk alongside the fence, steeply downhill, towards the tiny village of Clayton. At the foot of the descent go through a gate on to a chalky lane, which is often muddy and pitted by horses' hooves. On reaching the road, our route is to the right, but first, walk left to visit the remarkable church of St John Baptist. Notice the ripple marks on the rocks used for the path leading from the lych-gate to the church door.

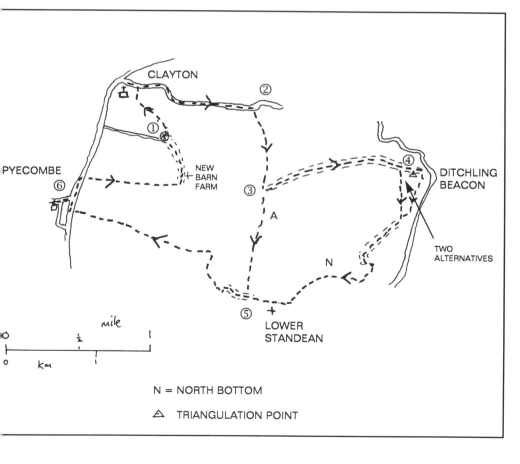

From the church retrace your steps along the road, passing the converted barn and the path we arrived on. Follow the narrow road for nearly a mile, through Clayton village. Here can be seen old buildings with flint, hung tiles and some clapboards, showing all the traditional building materials. Go on past the two sharp bends and then the pumping station for South East Water, noticing the steep scarp away to the right. We will soon have to climb this.

Turn right at a footpath sign to go through a small, wooden gate (2) by a large, iron gate. Climb steeply up between the bushes and small trees, on what might be a muddy path. On this climb look out for the deep coombe down to the right, with a wood, Clayton Holt, on the far side. Horses are numerous in this area and a few are likely to be grazing in the field down in the hollow. Birds are also numerous in this area.

The path leads up to join a stony track, which we follow to the top of the hill. Turn left along the South Downs Way (3) and walk eastwards.

If taking the short cut (A), after a few metres turn right alongside a fence and follow the field boundary southwards, downhill, for about three-quarters of a mile, to the buildings of Lower Standean Farm. Then continue the walk as described later.

For the main walk, continue eastwards on the hilltop, with the steep scarp to the left, and the more gentle dip slope to the right, cut by several deep dry valleys. After just over a mile, we approach Ditchling Beacon with a triangulation point at 813ft (248 metres), the highest point in East Sussex. Just before the Beacon we reach the Keymer Post on the Downland Circular Walk, where Heathy Brow is pointed off to the right, and Ditchling Beacon straight ahead. We are turning right just before reaching the car park, but go on to the car park (4) first if it is a hot day, as there may be an ice cream van waiting to serve you.

For the alternative route from the car park and its information board, instead of retracing your steps along the South Downs Way, go left across the grassy area to the patch of small trees. A path leads through this to a farm field, where a path heads across an open field, with the road clearly visible to the left. The path is almost parallel to the road. When you reach a track, turn right to walk away from the road and continue to the end of this field, where we will meet the other path already mentioned near the Keymer Post. Turn left to go down the grassy track.

For anyone not going on to Ditchling Beacon and the car park, the right turn mentioned above, will lead to a narrow, grassy path across open fields, on to an exposed and windswept piece of farmland. Reach an iron gate but keep straight on, with a fence on our left. As the path begins to descend, it merges with a track coming through a gate on the left. The track begins to descend, to be joined by a path from the left, which is an alternative route we might have taken from the Beacon car park.

We are now heading southwards and gently downhill into a dry valley. This is the blue route towards Heathy Brow. At the bottom turn right through a gate into North Bottom, which leads round to the left towards Lower Standean Farm. Before reaching the farm, move across to the right side of the dry valley, pass through a gate by a drinking trough, and follow a track to climb diagonally up the side of the valley. This leads up to the right, and then down to the left through a gate, to pass beyond the farm buildings.

Once past the farm there is a right turn along the hedge (5), which is where the **short cut** mentioned earlier **(A)** will join the main walk.

Continue the main walk from here by keeping straight on, to pass to the right of a flint and brick barn where swallows nest in summer. Go through a small gate into the next field then turn sharp left and follow this field boundary. Pass a water trough then turn right, but you are still following the fence. Keep going on to the far side of the field, where the fence turns right, and along here we will soon reach a gate.

Once through the gate, turn left and walk straight ahead to go across two fairways of the Pyecombe Golf Course and through two small patches of woodland. Pass another gate to descend to the road and magnificent views of Pyecombe, with its houses and the outstanding church and its Sussex cap.

A garage and pub (The Plough) are to the left, but we turn right here. Proceed for about 100 metres, and then turn left up School Lane to the village. The village church (6) is dedicated to the Transfiguration of Our Lord. The churchyard has an unusual tapsel gate, and a good seat for a picnic. Opposite the church is the house where the famous Pyecombe shepherds' crooks were made.

Retrace your steps through the village and turn left, following the South Downs Way signpost. Go along the road (A273), then cross over on to the Pyecombe Golf Course, which is really magnificent. A well-worn track leads us up the hill to the top of the golf course, where we turn left at a cross-paths to walk past New Barn Farm. Although on the top of the climb, the buildings are sheltered in a hollow and the farm is surrounded by a windbreak of trees. Many horses are likely to be seen in the stables and in the fields as we proceed along the path towards Jack and Jill. Jack, the black mill, is prominent, with the white sails of Jill behind. Admire the excellent views to the left of the windmills, looking north-westwards across the Weald to the sandstone hills in the background which are part of the ridge extending from Leith Hill and Pitch Hill.

A clear track leads back to the car parking area. An information board will be seen just before reaching the entrance, and an even larger information board is located in the car park. Here you will find an explanation of the dew ponds – there are several in this area. They are a traditional feature of the downs, used from medieval times until the 1930s for the large flocks of sheep which used to be so common on these chalk hills.

October: West Hoathly and Wakehurst

This walk is a circuit from West Hoathly to Wakehurst, passing over farmland and through woodland, especially the magnificent Wakehurst Gardens and Arboretum. Several small river valleys are crossed, which give short but steep slopes, and can often be muddy at this time of year. Members of the National Trust could start the walk at Wakehurst Arboretum. If you are a member, remember to take your membership ticket with you.

Moorhen

Distance: 8 – 9 miles, or 6 miles if not walking around Wakehurst.

Time: 4 hours, though more time could be spent in the arboretum.

Terrain: Undulating, mostly sheltered in woods or in valleys.

Maps: Landranger 187 or Explorer 135.

Starting Point: West Hoathly, GR 365327, reached from the B2028 going north from Haywards Heath or by the B2110 from East Grinstead.

Access: Buses run from East Grinstead and Crawley to West Hoathly.

Refreshments: Available in West Hoathly.

Nearest Towns: Haywards Heath, East Grinstead and Crawley

Nearest Tourist Information Centre: Horsham (01403 211661). Tourist information point in East Grinstead library (01342 410050).

Weather

The autumnal month of October can give brief flashbacks to the summer, or glimpses of wintry conditions ahead, and probably a sample of both. October 1994 was a typical month. Unsettled Atlantic conditions prevailed early and late in the month, with a sunny, settled spell in the middle producing a few days of Indian summer, named after the Indians of North America. The settled spell was a time of high pressure, often accompanied by mist and fog, as well as dew or even frost. This type of settled weather will not bring rain, and the well-known piece of weather lore – 'when the dew is on the grass, rain will never come to pass' – is particularly relevant, and a shrewd piece of observation by the originator of the comment. The alternative to high pressure weather is a low pressure system, when it is possible for south-westerly winds to bring mild nights and warm days, but rain is likely. In some particularly mild spells it has been known for spring flowers to bloom, as in 1995, having been misled by exceptionally mild temperatures. Occasional severe storms occur, and these are most frequent in the north of Scotland, but the notorious storm of 1987 was mainly felt in south-east England, on the morning of Friday the 16th. In addition to causing loss of life and huge amounts of structural damage, millions of trees were blown down. It has now been realised that nature is able to recover from loss of trees, and most areas of woodland have seen renewed growth to compensate for the damage and devastation in 1987.

The Countryside

The patchwork of fields in the countryside is at its most varied at this time of year, with most crops having been harvested and some fields already ploughed for the next planting. Others have stubble, which has increased in recent years since burning has been stopped. Flocks of small birds, notably larks, pipits and finches, as well as a few larger birds, jackdaws and rooks, are seeking food in the stubble. The green of the trees and hedges is being replaced by yellows and browns as the autumnal colours appear, and bare branches steadily increase during the month. Laurie Lee described this in *Cider with Rosie* as 'the trees are collapsing'. Many of the hedges will have been trimmed back, quite viciously in some cases. Where this has not happened there may be fruits and berries, providing a good source of food for birds, and some animals, as they build up reserves of fat for the winter months ahead. Beech mast, hazel nuts, and berries on elder, holly and hawthorn will be evident in places, as will red rosehips, and possibly the purple berries of belladonna. In the grassy fields the farm animals will still be seen, although this walk passes through only a few farm fields. On sunny days a few butterflies appear, and swarms of insects, too, though not resembling the hot and steamy days of August, when insects can become a nuisance to anyone out walking. If the weather is wet, it is worth looking out for the fungi which spring up rapidly, in all sizes and colours. Especially early in the day, walkers may encounter spiders' webs across the paths, and magnificent webs in the bushes and hedgerows, clearly seen if moistened by early morning dew clinging to the miles of thread.

Wakehurst Place

The 187-hectare (462-acre) estate became a branch of the Royal Botanic Gardens at Kew in 1965. This was to help relieve congestion at Kew, and because it is located in a less polluted atmosphere. 69 hectares (170 acres) are now open to the public throughout the year, with 40 hectares (100 acres) of garden, and the remainder as woodlands. These contain trees from America, Europe, Australia and Asia. Adjacent to the gardens is the Loder Valley Reserve.

Wakehurst Place

Owned by the Wakehurst family from the 12th to the 15th century, the estate then passed to the Culpepers, and it was Sir Edward Culpeper who built the present mansion in 1590, using local sandstone. The last Culpeper sold the estate in 1694, and it was occupied by several other families until bought in 1903 by Gerald Loder, who later became Lord Wakehurst. He developed the gardens, which are now attractive in all seasons, especially in spring and autumn, with a variety of habitats including the lakes, bogs and woodlands. It was bequeathed to the National Trust in 1963, and they lease it to the Royal Botanic Gardens, Kew. Paths allow visitors to wander all over these beautiful gardens.

The house contains an interesting exhibition, as well as a shop (not National Trust) and restaurant. The exhibition gives information about Wakehurst, including the fact that it has an average rainfall of 821mm of rain, quite high for south-eastern England. The rainfall, the geology and soils influence which plants can grow well here.

Loder Valley Reserve

A botanical reserve for Wealden vegetation, it also attracts birds, butterflies and insects. The reserve occupies 60 hectares (150 acres) of the Wakehurst Place estate, and is managed as a conservation area. Access for walkers is possible, once permission has been obtained from the Administrator at Wakehurst Place. At least 24 hours notice is required (tel. 01444 894066). It was mainly a woodland area, but the bottom part of one valley was flooded by Ardingly Reservoir, created by the Southern Water Authority in 1978, and provided an additional habitat. There are now rich collections of woodland, wetland and meadowland plants.

West Hoathly

A major attraction here is the museum in the Priest House, a 15th-century timber wattle and daub building, which was originally a farmhouse. It has been used as a museum since 1908, and contains furniture and household items, and has an interesting herb garden. House and garden are open 1st March until 31st October, 11am until 5.30pm, but only 2pm to 5pm on Sundays. There is an admission charge.

The 13th-century church of St Margaret is quite large, and has a tower with broach spire. Some cast-iron tombs (1619 and 1624) date from the time of the Sussex iron industry. Opposite the church, the old, tile-hung Combers has a plaque on the wall which reads, 'The Manor of the Rectory of West Hoathly held by Queen Elizabeth I, 1558, This sign was erected to commemorate the coronation of Queen Elizabeth II.' Also opposite the church is the Cat Inn.

The Walk

From the car park in Finche Field (1), which was given for the enjoyment of the public, walk towards the church. Take great care walking along the narrow road. It passes between houses and then goes up the hill near the church. When the road bends left, go straight across to a stile opposite The Cat Inn. Go over this to a track which leads past a house and becomes a path leading to a stile. Go on over this and along the field margin, with a hedge on the right. Pass a

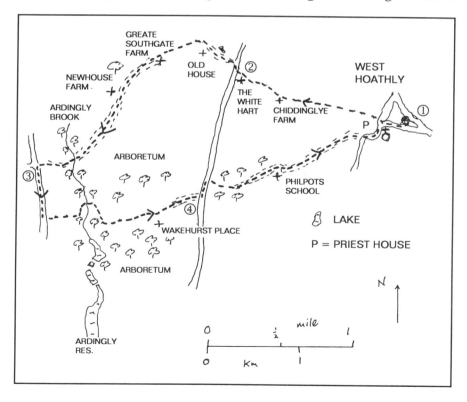

small pond in a clump of trees and keep ahead over the stile located between two metal gates. Continue straight along the field, again with a hedge on the right. A driveway comes through this hedge on the right to join our route. At the end of this field go over the stile (or through the gate), on to a surfaced driveway. Keep straight on until the drive splits just before the farm buildings.

Fork right here along a stony track, ignoring the first path on the right, passing the barns on our left, and beginning to descend. Go right through a metal kissing gate. This stony path leads down between bushes, trees and undergrowth to reach a stile, where we turn left along the margin of a grassy field. Note the holly trees on the left, and a grassy slope up to our right. Follow the left margin of this field, and then swing right, still following the margin, to reach a stile on our left. Go over this into a small patch of woodland, cross a footbridge and follow the path through the trees to reach a track. Turn left here over a stream, and begin to climb. The track degenerates to a path as we climb up to a brick stile and the B2028 (2).

The White Hart Inn, dating from the 14th century, is a few metres to the left if required, but we turn right for 20 metres, then left across the road on to the driveway to Old House. Pass between two ponds, with moorhens and ducks. Just beyond the drive on the left leading to Old House, look for the footpath sign and the path going left between hedges. Just before turning here, ahead and to the right can be seen the tall, brick watertower on Selsfield Common.

The path goes down steeply to a stile and across a small field. You reach two more stiles and a footbridge, to the left of which is a stone bridge, in the gardens near the tennis court. Cross another small field to a stile, and then pass to the right of a cattle trough and ascend slightly to reach the next stile. Cross the middle of the field (where the view back clearly shows the brick water tower again), following the telegraph wires and passing close to a lone oak and small clump of Scots pine. At the far side are two stiles in quick succession, then a small field and another stile. Next reach Great Strudgate Farm on our left, and a surfaced driveway.

Walk along this driveway for just over a mile, passing to the left of the main buildings of Newhouse Farm. There is a path leading off left here, but we keep straight ahead along the concrete drive. Pass a lake on the right, and then a house and barns before reaching a minor road (3). Turn left along Paddockhurst Road, following the signpost towards Balcombe and Ardingly. Walk along the road and climb gently, passing Square Wood on the left. You may notice a path on the right, and a few metres beyond this a path to the left, our route into Wakehurst. Go over the stile and walk along the field margin, with a house to our right. Bend left with the field margin and reach a metal kissing gate. Turn right down to a large gate, and go on steeply downhill, descending a gullied path, with a handrail to assist if required on the steepest stretch. Cross a small, plank footbridge, then a proper bridge over the main stream (Ardingly Brook). Begin to climb. The path bends right, but is clear and easy to follow. It crosses a small stream and climbs further, to reach a wooden walkway and then a large metal gate. This is the entry to Wakehurst Gardens. There is a public right of way crossing the arboretum, but walkers cannot stray from this path. Do admire the magnificent tree just through the gate, the first tree on the left. This majestic tree is a wellingtonia, sequoiadendron giganteum from California.

Cross the surfaced path and go straight along the public footpath ahead, up the grassy slope and through an area of bracken to a stile at the top. Go over here and along the narrow path through metal gates and between fences. There are likely to be deer in the fields on either side. Keep going between these fields to reach the buildings of Havelock Farm, and then on the left will be seen the Millennium Seed Bank. The MSB has been established to safeguard the entire flora of the United Kingdom and 10% of the world's plants, including many endangered species.

The driveway continues out to the main road, but notice the signpost pointing right, to the exit and car park (4). This information is for visitors to the arboretum, and if you are intending to take the extension walk around the arboretum, it is necessary to go and pay, unless you are a member of the National Trust. In either case, go up to the main entrance and obtain a map of Wakehurst, which will be helpful. It is well worth a visit, and although much of it can be seen in an hour or so, two to three hours will enable a fuller tour to be made. There is a restaurant and shop.

Extension Walk (Wakehurst Gardens)

With a map of the gardens and woodland, it is possible to walk wherever you wish, and for as long as you wish. However, this one-hour circuit sees as much as possible in that time. Pass between the shop and small kiosk, with the mansion down to the right. Notice the pond on the left as you walk slightly downhill to reach a cross-paths. (A signpost points right, to the exhibition and shop.) Go alongside the Asian Heath garden, with the large pool, Mansion Pond, on our right. Ducks and moorhens are numerous on the pond.

At the end of the pond follow the sign to The Slip, Water Garden, Westwood Valley and the Lake. Go down a few steps, following a small stream, and we are now on the valley side, with a steep valley down to the right. Follow the signpost towards the Wetland Conservation Area, and soon reach the seat and information boards, where a fine view looks out across part of Ardingly Reservoir and the Loder Valley. Ignore the public footpath sign just outside the boundary fence and carry on downhill, passing a wooden building used as a Study Centre. Reach a Wetland Conservation Information Board and walk on through the wetland area, with Westwood Lake to the right and the Ardingly Reservoir to the left.

Cross the broadwalk through the swampland area, with dragonflies in abundance, and start the return journey along the far side of Westwood Lake. Pass along the left side of the lake and then bear right across a wooden bridge and walkway. The main path soon bends left, following the signs to Bloomers Wood and Bethlehem Valley. Keep going along the gravel path, through an American area with huge sequoia and Douglas fir, and passing the public footpath we walked along earlier, which enters the gardens through a large, iron gate.

We are still heading towards Bethlehem, but when the path splits take the right fork to the Rock Walk, and pass through some huge outcrops of sandstone. Now start to follow the Way Out signs, and soon leave the woods. The path leads to a driveway to Havelock Farm. Signs refer to the footpath to Forest Ridge, which goes alongside the buildings, and there is a red arrow for the High Weald Circular Walk.

We come on to the main driveway and the path to West Hoathly is along this driveway and out to the road. However, signposted to the right is the path to the entrance and the car park, which is where the circuit of the arboretum began.

Main Walk continued

Walk along the driveway, with the new seed bank to the left. Pass between more deer in paddocks and the Wakehurst Place car park to the right. At the road, turn left and walk along the grassy verge for about 200 metres. Cross over and follow the bridleway sign between the two houses with hung tiles, and begin to go downhill. Go along the narrow path through mixed woodlands, with some larch as well as deciduous trees showing the golden colour of autumn. Reach a broader track and turn left, continuing downhill, and when the track divides, fork right. At the next cross-paths, just before reaching a small lake, turn left between clumps of bamboo, and walk along the left side of the small lakes, possibly with the noise of moorhens drifting through the bamboo jungle.

Cross over the stream, with the regulatory falls on the left, and begin to climb up the other side of the valley. Like all deep valleys at this time of year, it may be muddy. You may notice the outcrops of rock on the other side of the valley, and there are others like this in other valleys, most notably in part of Wakehurst Gardens. Near the top of the hill the track divides, and we fork right, which is really the continuation of our path. We pass between a few buildings and through a farmyard, then turn left along the track. Pass Philpots Manor School and keep going along the stony drive. This becomes surfaced as we approach houses and then reach a surfaced road.

We keep straight ahead along this road, with West Hoathly Bowling Club on our right, and soon pass the Priest House and the church, where we turn right to return to our starting point.

November: Singleton

A circuit from the village of
Singleton up on to the
Downs and round the
periphery of the Goodwood
racecourse, passing
through woods, farmland
and the tiny village of
Charlton on the way. Views
are quite stunning.

Goldfinch

Distance: 6 miles, with a short cut to 5 miles. Extra distance will be walked if a visit to the Open Air Museum is included in the day out.

Time: About 3 hours

Terrain: Clear paths of chalk and flint, which can be hard on the feet unless boots are worn. Just one climb is involved, but no really steep hills, though the chalk areas often become muddy and slippery after rain has fallen.

Maps: Landranger 197 and Explorer 120.

Starting Point: Singleton village, GR 877132, although spacious alternatives are in the car park alongside the road at the foot of the Trundle (GR 878114) or outside the main entrances to the racecourse (GR 886111).

Access: Chichester has a railway station and a regular bus service running to Midhurst via Singleton.

Refreshments: Pubs in Singleton or Charlton, with a snack bar alongside the road near the Trundle.

Nearest Town: Chichester, which has a Tourist Information Centre (tel. 01243 775888).

Weather

Although cold spells often occur in November, much of the month is generally mild though wet and windy. The main path of the Atlantic depressions, which bring our wettest weather, is along the western fringes of Britain, passing just across northern Scotland. This often allows humid, southerly air to drift into south-east England, ideal for the formation of fog. Fogs are quite common in November, and with little heat in the sun, they can be persistent. Fogs and rain contribute to a damp feel in the month and it is the time when fields and footpaths become wet, so be prepared. The need for adequate waterproof footwear will continue through until next Easter. Severe cold is unusual in November, though frosts do occur. The first sharp frosts generally result in the last of the leaves falling from the deciduous trees, though until mid-month there are generally impressive autumnal colours. The grass has stopped growing, and most of the dairy cattle will have gone indoors. This means they will not be standing around on public footpaths, which always seem to be their favourite grazing locations. Is the grass better where it has been trodden by boots, or do they just like the company?

'A cold November, a warm Christmas,' says the old saying. It may turn out to be true, but there is no direct link between the weather at these two periods.

The Countryside

The countryside is closing down for the winter, but there is always something to see whilst out walking. The trees and hedges are looking bare, though the last fruits and berries may still be available for hungry birds. Thick hedges and some areas of dense undergrowth are invaluable for birds, as are the coniferous forests, although not all varieties of birds make use of these. Pheasants and partridges are quite numerous in the area of this walk, flocks of finches are foraging in the fields, and groups of skylarks, too. In the woodland areas there are flocks of tits, touring around from one tree to the next, though they are often helped in their quest for food by kind householders and the food they leave out in gardens. The open hills often support flocks of birds in the winter (although November is still part of autumn), and kestrels will be hovering around, searching for a mouse or vole. Fields are often bare after ploughing, but many fields have the first few inches of next year's crops, often with skylarks, pigeons, rooks scouring the ground for food. A few downland areas have fields of set-aside, where flowers and weeds will attract flocks of finches. These will include goldfinches, which make a twittering noise almost like the tinkling of a bell. The group name for these birds is most appropriate: they are referred to as a 'charm' of goldfinches. Rooks and gulls will be following tractors if ploughing is taking place, and where muck spreading is the main activity, many birds are investigating the possibilities of food.

Singleton

One of the most picturesque villages in the South Downs, though different from many in that it is not situated at the foot of the escarpment. It has grown up on the dip slope, in a fairly deep valley eroded by what is now the tiny River Lavant, flowing south into Chichester Harbour. An old village, which is mentioned in the Domesday Book, Singleton has been important for centuries, but had a surge of activity after 1801, when Goodwood Racecourse was opened. The village was crowded with racegoers (including royalty). Rowdy behaviour became a problem as racegoers had to stay in the local villages before the days of motor travel. Sporting hooliganism is not just a modern development associated with football matches! The older cottages in the village are mostly flint and brick, and date from the 17th or 18th centuries. One or two still have thatch, and roses grow round some of the windows. There are many colourful gardens, a duck pond and a cricket pitch. The village also has two 18th-century pubs, so why not have a lunch before setting off on the walk.

The Church of St John the Evangelist in Singleton

This ancient church dates from around AD975, and has links with Earl Godwin – 'Godwin's Wood' became 'Goodwood'. He was the father of King Harold, who achieved fame at Battle in 1066. The church is still much the same in design as it was in his day, and the tower and nave walls are definitely Saxon. Changes and additions have been made over the centuries. For example, the tower arch, which was originally Saxon, was given a pointed arch in the 13th century. The fine Perpendicular aisle windows date from about 1400, and the pews from about 1450. The door halfway up the tower and the window above the chancel arch are thought to be evidence of an upper room above the nave, which was possibly used by visiting priests. There are three windows in the tower to let in the maximum amount of light. The double window high up in the nave is also interesting: it was made with remains of medieval glass. The kneelers are wonderful pieces of needlework, made by local parishioners in the 1980s. The Caen stone reredos has a carving of the Last Supper. On leaving the church, notice the medieval graffiti on the door posts, relics of pilgrims passing this way.

Trundle Hill

Formerly the location of a chapel, the outstanding features on the hill now are the masts and the massive mounds of the camp created by Neolithic man about 2500BC. They used flints as tools, and had developed the arts of weaving and pottery by that time. Subsequently, the Iron Age Celts used it as a fort, about 300BC, and the Romans also used this dramatic hilltop site.

Goodwood Racecourse

This most picturesque course was opened by the 3rd Duke of Richmond in 1801. At that time, many of the visitors would stay in the nearby villages. From 1880 to 1935 it was possible to travel here by train on the Midhurst to Chichester railway line, which stopped at Singleton Station. The line was closed for passenger traffic in 1935, but continued to see a few goods trains until 1954. The Prince of Wales (Edward VII) kept his horses in the Singleton stables, and he was a regular visitor. He first used the expression 'glorious Goodwood' and considered his visits to be a garden party with a race tacked on. This is still relevant for some people today. If you wish to have a quiet walk it is best to avoid a race day.

Charlton

This tiny village was the home of one of Britain's most famous hunts in the 18th century. Fox Hall was built as a hunting lodge by the Duke of Richmond in 1732. With its tall chimneys, it still looks very impressive. Along the track from Fox Hall is the sawmill, which makes use of some of the local supplies of timber.

Charlton

Weald and Downland Open Air Museum

Founded by J.R. Armstrong and a group of enthusiasts in 1967, this has steadily grown and is well worth a visit, though 2 to 3 hours will be required for a complete tour of the museum. First opened in 1971, this museum has a collection of more than 30 vernacular buildings from south-east England, which were saved from destruction and were rebuilt here. It is a non-profit-making organisation, and much of the work is done by volunteers. The site occupies 16 hectares (40 acres) of beautiful downland, which was given by Edward James who lived in West Dean House. The museum is open daily from March to October, but in winter opens on Wednesdays and at week-ends, from 10.30am to 4pm.

The Walk

Leave the churchyard (1) by a gate at the south-west corner. Pass Manor Farm on the right, go over a stile and up the hill. There are numerous red-legged partridges around here, including some in the churchyard, but their days are numbered as many are likely to be shot this month. A few flowers might still add colour to the path if the month has been mild. Across the dry valley to the right is the road from Singleton to Goodwood, with autumnal colours in the wood just beyond.

As we climb up the flinty track, pause to admire the views to the left, right and behind. The old part of Singleton can be recognised by

Red-legged Partridge

the housing styles and building materials. The church and the fine buildings of Manor Farm are outstanding, but the large barns of the farm are the least attractive parts of the village landscape. It is interesting to see how farm buildings have often been able to escape from the kind of planning controls which affect other buildings. Dotted all around in the surrounding countryside are patches of woodland, especially on the higher ground. These clearly show the change of the seasons, with autumnal colours as well as some bare trees.

Once at the top of the hill, views open out ahead, with the racecourse and the grandstand, as well as Trundle Hill, showing up clearly. Walking through the fields, many of which have normally been cropped for cereals in recent years, there may be pheasants running around, as well as partridges. Skylarks flutter around in this area too, and their twittering may be heard. By the end of the field the path levels off, and we climb a stile and then head diagonally left across the next field.

Climb the stile and turn right along the minor road, leading gradually uphill and heading towards the masts on top of the Trundle. Cross the main road (2) at the car park, where there might be a refreshment van. Pass the Trundle enclosure, a spectators' area for the racecourse, on our left and climb steeply up the last 150ft (45 metres) to the triangulation point at 676ft (206 metres). Correctly named St Roche's Hill, this was the location of St Roche's Chapel, which was attached to Singleton Church many years ago.

The views all round would have enabled earlier inhabitants to spot any approaching enemies, but now it is just a delightful location for admiring Chichester Cathedral and the coastline indented with glistening inlets, one of which reaches to the Roman port of Fishbourne, with the Isle of Wight in the background. A windmill is visible on Halnaker Hill, three miles to the south-east, but there used to be a windmill on the Trundle, too, until it was struck by lightning in 1790 and two men were killed. They are buried in Singleton churchyard. Other deaths have occurred on the Trundle as it was the site for the gallows until 1791 – when that was also struck by lightning.

Leave the hill by a path alongside the iron railings, heading in the direction of the main racecourse buildings, and go down through an area of mixed woodlands. The trees include beech, spindle, yew and Mediterranean oak, and there are rose hips and blackberries in the undergrowth. Spindle will be showing off its segmented, reddish pink fruit, which with remnants of reddish leaves make it an outstanding shrub at this time of year. It is the only British woody plant to have promising properties for insecticide as well as being a source of dyes.

As we walk alongside the racecourse buildings, look down to the right at the attractive golf course in a dry valley, and the spire of Chichester Cathedral in the background. Turn left along the Petworth road, still following the margins of the racecourse. The large expanse of picnic and parking space on the right of the road becomes very crowded in summer, especially on race days. The Country Park is in the Goodwood Estate down to the right. The last building on the left is the children's playground, in which no adults are allowed,

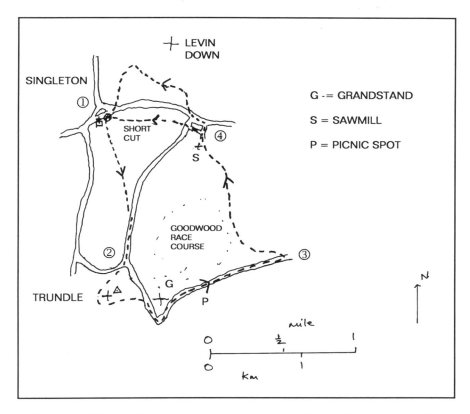

and then a flint wall separates the road from the main straight of the race track. Just imagine the thundering hooves on race days as they speed down towards the grandstand.

At the end of the straight, leave the road (3) and turn sharp left along a track which follows the racecourse margin, cutting through the woods of Charlton Park, rich in plant life. Ragwort, herb robert, daisies and coltsfoot may still be in flower, and a variety of trees and abundance of birds help to make this walk of interest for nature lovers. Pheasants are particularly loud, and they strut around in a noisy and arrogant fashion. Other bird noises will include the muttering of red-legged partridges, and twittering of finches and tits. The racecourse is still on the left, but this is the 'out in the country' section of the track, and contains a sharp bend known as 'accident corner'. Our walk follows the path leading down to the tiny village of Charlton,

and as the views open out we see a dry valley to the right and delightful countryside across the Lavant Valley. Green fields of pasture al-
ternate with ploughed land where the young shoots of next year's
cereals give a thin green cover.

The village, now part of Singleton parish, is a mixture of old, flint
houses and more modern, brick structures. Fox Hall was built in
1732 as a hunting lodge for the 2nd Duke of Richmond. The Charlton Hunt used to be based here, and would gather on Levin Down,
but declined in importance when the 3rd Duke of Richmond kept
his horses at Goodwood House. The greatest activity in the village
nowadays is at the sawmill, Downland Fencing, which is passed on
the left before reaching Fox Hall.

Short Cut

Just beyond Fox Hall is the War Memorial on the right (4). The short-
est route back to Singleton involves turning left here, to walk along
the road between houses. At the end of the houses, cross over the minor road which leads up to the Trundle. Go over the stile and across
the middle of a very stony field, passing marker posts conveniently
placed to show the path. Head westwards across two fields and then
straight on between houses to head directly to the church in Singleton.

Longer Route

The main walk back to Singleton keeps straight ahead at the war memorial. At the T-junction, where the magnificent, flint farm building
is on the right, we turn left. Pass the Fox Inn and the Hunting Lodges.
The Fox is 18th century. Next to it are twin hunting lodges connected by a gateway. They were built at the same time as Fox Hall for
the use of the Duke of Devonshire and Lord Harcourt. Since then the
lodges have been used as a farm. There is an old granary, but all the
buildings have been modernised.

Pass the narrow road on the right and the narrow but wider road
on the left, signposted Goodwood 1 mile. One hundred metres further along the road, go right over the stile and across the field. At the
top of the field, go over two stiles and reach an information board
about Levin Down. The board mentions the old, chalk grassland
which has escaped ploughing, allowing grasses and flowers to flour-
ish. One of the special flowers here is the round-headed rampion,
also known as the Pride of Sussex, though it also grows on the North

Downs and on downland in Hampshire and Wiltshire. This area is a nature reserve owned by the Goodwood Estate, but managed by the Sussex Wildlife Trust since 1981. Much scrub has grown on the hill, and volunteer workers have cleared many young hawthorn trees and other bushes. Sheep have also been grazed here to help control the scrub.

The map on the board shows several footpaths and it is possible to walk right around the hill if required, but we go left on the side of Levin Hill, from where we can admire the views of the Trundle and the main stand on the racecourse. Cross through an area of grass, scrub and bushes, where masses of rose-hips may be seen. Pass a small stile on the left, and a few metres beyond this is a large gate with a stile alongside. Go straight on through here, across a wide open field, with views to the right as well as the left. Before reaching

Weald and Downland Open Air Museum

the fence at the far side of the field, turn left on the bridleway which has come right round Levin Hill.

Turn left towards a gate at the bottom corner of the field. About 45 metres to the left of this gate is a stile. Go over this to descend steeply through the stony field – still covered in stubble when last walking here, on a glorious, sunny day in mid-November. In view from this field were grass, new plough, young crops and old stubble – the full range of possibilities for land use. The path leads down to a grassy track alongside the school, and out to the road. Turn right, passing the village hall on the left, and walk back towards the church. In Singleton is the Fox and Hounds, dating from the 16th century, when it was owned by the Fitzalan family, Earls of Arundel. It was probably closed in the late 18th century but reopened in the 1840s, and was, and still is, very popular on race days. Excellent food is available for walkers, as well as motorists.

From the village, if you have more time available, walk along the main road and pay a visit to the Weald and Downland Open Air Museum.

December: Hartfield

This walk through woods and across farmland comprises a circuit through part of Ashdown Forest, in what is known as Pooh territory. It passes through 100 Aker Wood (now called 500 Acre Wood) and crosses over Pooh Bridge. It is a trip down memory lane for many fans of Winnie the Pooh.

Bracken

Distance: 9½ miles, with a short cut route of 7 miles.

Time: 4 (or 3) hours

Terrain: Flat or gently undulating, but with several potentially muddy locations.

Maps: Landranger 188 or Explorer 135.

Starting Point: The main street or near the church in Hartfield, parking is available along the main road GR 477355. Hartfield is located at the crossroads of the B2026 and B2110, just south of the A264 East Grinstead to Tunbridge Wells road.

Access: Railway station at East Grinstead, bus services link East Grinstead with Hartfield.

Refreshments: Available in Hartfield and at the pub in Withyham.

Nearest Town: Crowborough

Nearest Tourist Information Centre: East Grinstead (tel. 01342 410050)

Weather

The south-east of England has an average of less than ten days a year with snow lying on the ground, compared with over 40 days on the Pennines and the hills of Wales. As walkers know only too well, height makes a great difference to the amounts of snow: for every 100 metres of height, about five more days of snow can be expected in England and Wales. Cold weather mostly comes from the north or east, though in December this is not generally as cold as in the other winter months of January or February. The sea temperature is still about 10°C in the Channel and North Sea, so can warm up cold winds coming towards Britain. Cold weather is associated with anti-cyclonic conditions, and it was these in the past that caused the infamous smogs. In the Great Smog of London, 5th to 9th December 1952, more than 4000 people died. Since the Clean Air Act of 1956, severe smogs have not occurred.

December is also likely to experience one or more spells of westerly weather, and is generally the least sunny month of the year. This is partly because of short days, but also because of the frequency of cloudy weather.

The Countryside

'A green Christmas brings a heavy harvest,' implies that a mild Christmas is good for crops. This is not necessarily true, as spring and summer weather is not related to the weather at Christmas. Certain cereal crops will already be growing but they have two more months of wintry weather to survive, with little growth possible. These crops are ready to shoot up when warmer conditions really arrive, and will ripen earlier than crops planted in the spring – and hence earn more money for the farmer. With the possible increase in winter temperatures due to global warming, there are likely to be more crops planted in the autumn. Other fields are still fallow or perhaps covered with stubble. Wild birds are scouring fields and hedges for any scraps of food, but it is often a difficult period for them and they may be dependent on fat accumulated during the autumn when food was abundant. The death rate is very high, especially among the smaller birds. Their bodies do, however, provide food for the larger scavengers and carrion eaters. Although a quiet month for plant growth, there are the first signs of the green shoots for next year's spring flowers in the woods and in the gardens, and winter flowering trees are showing some blossom. Mistletoe and holly berries are seasonal attractions, but perhaps the brightest colour on wild plants is on gorse, which produces bright yellow flowers even in December. Many plants are still very brown with dead leaves from last autumn, but these do often contain insect life, and wrens and goldcrests are often seen searching every plant for tiny specks of food. Bracken may also attract larger birds, notably pheasants, which crash their way through the noisy bracken, and take off with a great whirring noise if disturbed. It is still the shooting season for pheasants and partridges, as well as ducks and geese, but grouse on the moors are safe from the 10th December.

Hartfield

A.A. Milne lived in Hartfield, and consequently there is a shop in the village, The Pooh Corner shop. It is located in a Tudor building and is open daily, selling a wide range of Pooh memorabilia. The origins of Hartfield were connected to Ashdown Forest and the hunting of the deer (hart). The church of St Mary the Virgin dates from the 13th century, the oldest remaining part being in the north wall. The tower and broach spire probably date from the 15th century, as does part of the Rectory, which, like the village school, is adjacent to the church. Many houses in the village date from the 16th to the 18th century.

Ashdown Forest

The ancient forest extends southwards from Hartfield to the west of Crowborough and as far as Maresfield. Two thousand years ago it was part of the dense, impenetrable forest which covered much of the Weald. The Romans named it the Forest of Anderida (Silva Anderida), but nowadays it is not all wooded. Much of the so-called forest is heathland, one of the largest areas of heathland remaining in England. Gorse, bracken and heather provide colour at different times of the year, and patches of beech, oak and pine add further variety to the landscape. The forest was formerly a hunting ground for kings, but many trees were removed in the 16th and 17th centuries to provide fuel for iron workings, as well as to make ships for the navy. Much is owned by the County Council, but is open to the public and is managed by a group of Conservators and the Forest Rangers. Amongst the wild life for which the forest is noted are the hobby

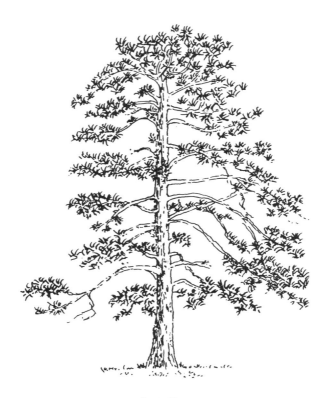

Scots Pine

and the rare Dartford Warbler. Many other warblers, nightjars and nightingales may be seen or heard in summer. The animal life includes deer and badgers, as well as adders, grass snakes and lizards – but these last three are not to be seen in December. Though the forest is now more heathland than forest, 40 per cent of the total area (of 2600 hectares, 6400 acres) is still wooded. Many trees have been recently planted, often in clumps. The different areas of forest are old mixed deciduous, beech woods, coppiced woods, recently developed beech wood areas, and the regions with Scots pines. Alder, yew, hazel and rowan are also found in several places. The variety of woodland, with the heathland, helps to provide diverse habitats for different forms of wild life. Most of the Ashdown Forest area is of sandstone, giving generally acidic soils. The sandstones are of the

Dartford Warbler

Ashdown Forest Beds, part of the Cretaceous period, and they contain both hard and soft sandstones, as well as sands rich in iron which gave rise to the old iron workings.

Withyham Church
The church of St Michael and All Angels dates from the 13th century but was mostly rebuilt by 1400, and rebuilt again after being destroyed by lightning in 1663. The sundial near the door is dated at 1672. The interior is dominated by the Sackville chapel, which lies above a vault where numerous coffins of the Sackville family have been placed. There are records of Sackville burials here since 1451. The monument in the middle of the chapel is by Cibber and is a memorial to Thomas Sackville, who died at the age of 13 in 1677. The boy holds a skull, an indication that he died before his parents, who are portrayed kneeling on the steps of the tomb. A genealogical window on the east wall shows the descent of the family from the Herbrand de Sauqueville who came over from Normandy with William the Conqueror. The other outstanding item in the church is the set of four 15th-century paintings relating to the Passion. They are on the south wall but are only copies as the originals are now in Leeds Castle for safer keeping.

The Walk

From the Pooh Corner shop (1), walk through the village along the main road, passing an interesting assortment of houses, two pubs and a tea shop. Just before the main road bends right towards Withyham and Tunbridge Wells, turn left along the track at the far end of the playing field, following the public bridleway sign. Pass to the right of the pavilion and along the field margin to reach the line of the old railway. Turn left and follow this easy route, stepping out at speed, although we may be overtaken by horses or bikes. Pass a cross-paths and a bench (too soon for a picnic!). After about 500 metres along here, go left down a few steps, through a gate, across a small field and through another gate into the woods. It may be muddy! The path emerges from the wood, and we just keep straight ahead, with views to the village over to the left. Pass Culvers Farm and a few houses and soon emerge on the road, opposite the drive to Landhurst.

Turn left along the road (2), and after about 200 metres turn right at a little concrete sign pointing up the drive to Hook Farm House. The route is through the gate with a yellow footpath arrow, and along a field margin. After a stile and a narrow field, go over two stiles, turning right along the field margin. Leave this field over a stile on to a driveway, and then go diagonally left over another stile. Walk downhill across two fields and two stiles to emerge on a narrow, surfaced road. After about 130 metres, go straight ahead to the left of the private road to Ryecroft Farm. Descend along a bridleway through Posingford Wood to Poohsticks Bridge.

The Pooh Bridge was built in 1907, but because it receives so many visitors it was in need of repair and was rebuilt in 1979. Walk straight on, after a game of Pooh sticks, up a broad and well-gullied path to a road. Turn left, and after 30 metres, when the road bends right, Andbell House is to the left. We go straight ahead, passing a sign indicating that horses should give way to walkers – quite right too - and follow the path through woods to emerge at a small car park called Poohsticks car park (3).

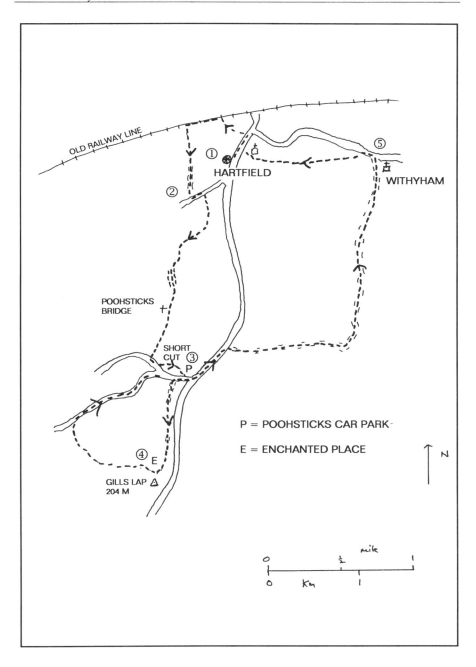

OLD RAILWAY LINE

① HARTFIELD

②

⑤

WITHYHAM

POOHSTICKS
BRIDGE

SHORT
CUT ③
P

④ E

GILLS LAP △
204 M

P = POOHSTICKS CAR PARK

E = ENCHANTED PLACE

N

mile

0   ½   1

0   Km   1

Poohsticks Bridge

Short Cut

For anyone wishing to walk the shorter alternative, leave the car park and turn left along the road. At the B2026, turn left again, towards Hartfield. Beyond the Forest Ridge House, turn right opposite a house called The Paddocks, and take a well-worn track into the woods. This is the Five Hundred Acre Wood, called 100 Aker Wood by Christopher Robin. Cross a footbridge over a small stream and keep straight ahead, heading eastwards. Pass an area of recent planting on the right before reaching a deer enclosure on the left and the gate to Kovacs Lodge. Go straight ahead along the surfaced road, climb a hill and pass a couple of houses on the left, then fork left at the split of the drive. After 20 metres follow a WW (Wealdway) footpath sign to the right of the drive, along the narrow path between fields which leads through to a narrow road. Pass the large complex of buildings at Buckhurst Farm, several houses of Fisher's Gate, and go on northwards to Withyham Church (5).

Lych Gate Cottage in Hartfield church yard

Go on down to the road – The Dorset Arms is to the right along the main road. Turn left then once over the bridge, go left over a high stile into a field. Go diagonally uphill past the edge of a wood, and on to the far corner of the field. Go over the stile and then diagonally through the next field, and over the next stile to follow the right margin of two fields. This leads through to the church of St Mary the Virgin in Hartfield. Pass the interesting old Lych-gate Cottage, thought to date from 1520, as we enter the churchyard. The cottage belonged to the Earls de la Warr until they gave it to the parish in 1956. Just beyond the church, pass the Anchor Inn on the right and the old pump (1831 and still working) on the left. Also on the left is the Hartfield Memorial Garden. As we turn left along the road, there are plaques to commemorate Hartfield's considerable successes in winning the best-kept small village competition in 1991 and 1992. A few metres along the road we reach the starting point.

Longer Route

For the longer walk to the Enchanted Place (2½ extra miles), turn right along the road from the car park. After about 80 metres, where a broad track comes out of the woods on the right, turn left along a track going into Ashdown Forest. The broad track leads between oak, silver birch and bracken, and begins to climb slowly, though becoming steeper. Keep going uphill, following the broad ride in a southerly direction and admiring the good views over to the right.

The broad ride splits at a point where there are two Scots pines and a memorial seat to Peter Dyball. The straight ahead track is becoming almost level, but we fork left with a slight dog-leg here then continue to climb steadily. Noise of traffic on the road to the left is likely to be heard, and some erosional gullies on exposed, steep slopes make this path uneven in places. As the track approaches the top of the hill (Gills Lap, 669ft, 204m), a broad track goes off to the right, which is our route ahead, but just beyond this is the Enchanted Place. It is in a circle of trees and the views to the north are spectacular (4).

On the plaque is the inscription:
'And by and by they came to an enchanted place on the very top of the forest called Galleons Lap.'

A.A. Milne (1882-1956) and E.H. Shepard (1879-1976) are commemorated at the Enchanted Place. They collaborated in the creation of Winnie the Pooh, and so captured the magic of Ashdown Forest and gave it to the world.

After admiring the views, continue the walk along the grassy track in a north-westerly direction. The track soon begins to bend round to the west and then a little south of west, with good views out to the right. There is not much greenery in December, though a little gorse is often in flower. Earlier in autumn there is a mass of heather around here.

Meet a large track going down to the right, and turn here to head in a north-westerly direction. Go downhill (with a view ahead towards a white house on the hill in the distance), passing the point where a broad track comes in from the left, and almost immediately another from the right. Keep straight ahead, and steadily downhill, in a north-westerly direction. Pass another track going off to the right. Soon after this the track splits. We keep left on the bigger branch, still descending and now heading westwards. After a track comes in from the left we begin to bend to the left. At the next split in the track, take the right turn and follow this down to a narrow road.

Turn right here and walk along this undulating road, past Jack Humphreys' farm and then The Rough on the right. Pass a small road turning off to the left and then the entrance to Spring Farm on the right. Continue past a few houses and then White House Farm on the left. Reach a road coming in from the left, and pass two large drives leading to houses on the right (Jumpers and Woodruff). Pass a broad track on the left, and the track on the right which we walked up earlier. After a few more metres reach the Poohsticks car park (3 again). Now follow the route of the shorter walk.

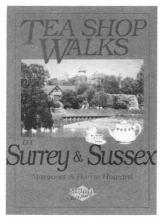

Also of interest:

TEA SHOP WALKS IN SURREY & SUSSEX
Margaret and Barrie Howard
This book of 26 walks takes the reader the length and breadth of the area, visiting popular towns and tiny villages. Each walk features a tea shop that welcomes walkers.
"An enjoyable mixture of rambling and relaxation ... this book offers a quintessentially English slice of life." SURREY ADVERTISER.
£6.95

WEST SUSSEX CHURCH WALKS
Diana Pé

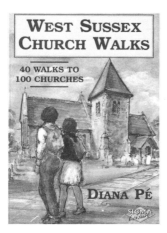

"The inspiration for this book sprung from a delight in wandering the downs and seeing in the distance an unpretentious church whose tower rises above a quiet hamlet." says Diana Pé. Let your mind wander back to the past as you walk down the same flint track down towards the same flint church in which shepherds, pedlars and other travellers sought refuge all those years ago. More than a walking guide, this book contains absorbing histories of each church which in turn reveal something of the skills, beliefs and religious fervour of people who lived up to 1000 years ago.
Her carefully planned walks range from 3 to 10 miles and cover a variety of terrain from coastal plains and woodland to meandering riversides and gently undulating hills. All are fully illustrated with sketch maps and photographs.
£7.95

All of our books are available through booksellers. In case of difficulty, or for a free catalogue, please contact: **SIGMA LEISURE, 1 SOUTH OAK LANE, WILMSLOW, CHESHIRE SK9 6AR.**
Phone: 01625-531035
Fax: 01625-536800.
E-mail: sigma.press@zetnet.co.uk .
Web site: http//www.sigmapress.co.uk

MASTERCARD and VISA orders welcome. Please add £2 p&p to all orders.